# INTERSTATE CUSTODY LITIGATION:

## A GUIDE TO USE AND COURT INTERPRETATION OF THE UNIFORM CHILD CUSTODY JURISDICTION ACT

# INTERSTATE CUSTODY LITIGATION:

## A GUIDE TO USE AND COURT INTERPRETATION OF THE UNIFORM CHILD CUSTODY JURISDICTION ACT

With text of the UCCJA, official commentary, case law analysis, and text and summary of similar federal legislation and international treaties.

By Richard E. Crouch, Managing Editor
of the Family Law Reporter

BNA

The Bureau of National Affairs, Inc.
Washington, D.C.

Library of Congress Catalog Number: 81-6082
International Standard Book Number: 0-87179-357-1
Printed in the United States of America

# TABLE OF CONTENTS

## THE FAMILY LAW REPORTER

This book was prepared with the assistance of the various editors and staff of the Family Law Reporter. A weekly publication of The Bureau of National Affairs, Inc., since 1974, the Family Law Reporter digests from slip opinions of all state and federal courts that issue written opinions those decisions of particular interest to family law practitioners which are too new to have appeared in advance sheets. The author, a member of the Virginia bar since 1964, has served as Managing Editor of the Family Law Reporter since its inception.

FLR takes special care to report all significant cases applying and interpreting the Uniform Child Custody Jurisdiction Act. For those interested in keeping up with UCCJA interpretations in the future, FLR subscription information is provided on the last page of this book.

# INTRODUCTION: THE UNIFORM CHILD CUSTODY JURISDICTION ACT

When the National Conference of Commissioners on Uniform State Laws drafted the Uniform Child Custody Jurisdiction Act in 1968, they announced that it was designed to: (1) avoid jurisdictional conflicts and promote cooperation between courts of different states, (2) provide for litigation to take place in the state with the "closest connection" to the child, (3) discourage continuing controversy by encouraging binding decisions, and (4) penalize parents for "abductions and other unilateral removals of children."

The Uniform Child Custody Jurisdiction Act is one of those legislative reforms that virtually everyone can feel good about. Though it has taken some time to make its way through the state legislatures since being drafted in 1968, no one seems ever to have articulated a reason for opposing its enactment. Because this statute seeks to minimize the incentives for interstate removal of children, and so thoroughly discourages litigation by the people who do it, it should go far toward improving the image of family law practice everywhere. The Act now enters a phase of its history in which it will be virtually universal law, and apparently operating in conjunction with a federal statute that requires observance of the Act by all states, and full faith and credit for custody decrees. Also in the background is the possibility of a U.S. Supreme Court ruling to require the same full faith and credit result.

Because nationwide popularity of the Uniform Act (UCCJA) has geometrically increased in recent years, so that almost all 50 states now have the Act, lawyers everywhere would do well to educate themselves about it. In most of the 44 states that have adopted the Act as of this writing, it is new and largely unconstrued legislation. In the few remaining states, lawyers should learn everything they can about the Act, because it will probably govern the return of children to, if not from, their state. Also, it is very likely to become law within the next one or two legislative sessions in those states. Finally the new federal anti-forum-shopping statute (the Wallop Amendment, PL 96-611 explained below) seeks to bind all states to observe the UCCJA by embodying its key sections in federal statutory law.

Custody litigation across state and national borders increased greatly in the 1970s, and in the 1980s there will probably be much more of it. It is partly that lawyers are more knowledgeable and imaginative, courts more receptive to new theories, and clients less willing to take a lawyer's no for an answer nowadays. Also, the very availability of new tools enabling a lawyer to attack problems that in earlier decades were considered hopeless for all but the wealthiest and most determined clients tends to multiply litigation.

The Uniform Child Custody Jurisdiction Act, which embodies the principles of comity, continuing jurisdiction, and forum non conveniens, should considerably improve the interstate practice of family law in many ways. First—and the importance of this advantage should not be overlooked—it puts the state's own principles of custody jurisdiction law in easily-located statutory form. Even though in most states the Act only codified principles that were already law, the research and courtroom debate over these uncodified principles of law consumed much energy. Worse yet, trial judges who only rarely see interstate custody cases have come up with some indefensible and disastrous rulings. It is understandable for a trial judge to take the position in all cases that the court can never assert jurisdiction over a child not physically present, or that personal jurisdiction over a parent allows the court to decide the custody of a child who has never in its life been present in the state—but the UCCJA sets forth the common-sense concepts of "home state" and "information availability" as jurisdictional bases so as to avoid such unjust results. It not only discourages forum-shopping, but also brings to the field a certainty of expectation about the other states' jurisdictional law that could never be counted on before. Obviously it makes counsel's task far easier when it is known that the foreign state's law is all contained in a concise code that is just the same as your own state's.

## PRE-ACT BACKGROUND

The Uniform Child Custody Jurisdiction Act can now be called a truly uniform nationwide law, since as of now, all states but Massachusetts, Mississippi, South Carolina, Texas, and the District of Columbia have enacted it—with enactment expected soon in these holdout states. Massachusetts has adopted the entire Act by Supreme Judicial interpretation of the existing state law, and Texas has very similar legislation. Before the Act gathered momentum and achieved such popularity in the past five years, the law of child custody jurisdiction produced some very unsatisfactory results. It was an area in which for the most part, conscientious judges did their best to assure fairness and safeguard children's welfare. But the climate created by the uncertainty about other states' law was one in which child-snatching, followed up by litigative attempts to legitimize it, flourished.

The law laid down by the U.S. Supreme Court for many years now has been that the Full Faith and Credit Clause of the U.S. Constitution necessarily cannot apply to custody orders, since they must always remain non-final if custody allocation is going to be based on the current best interest of a child. It was in fact the rule of most states, however, to extend comity to other states' decrees even though not required by federal authority to do so. The principles of continuing jurisdiction and forum non conveniens were also accepted by most states as governing interstate custody jurisdiction law. It had, in fact, become popular for courts to expressly apply the principles of the UCCJA in states that had not yet adopted it, on the ground that those principles were the better view anyway.

Often, however, the vain hope that a child-snatcher would move to a state that would then legitimize his or her custody encouraged child-snatching, even though the end result was that comity was accorded. Also, there remained some states in which judges took a very narrow states-rights view, reassessing current best interest of the child with a generous measure of prejudice for the now-local litigant, and theorized broader exceptions to the general rule of comity than the UCCJA allows.

## WHAT IT DOES

For the most part, the UCCJA—like the Wallop Amendment if it is held constitutional—is going to moot this prior body of law, so that it will no longer be helpful to cite U.S. Supreme Court cases in arguing custody jurisdiction. The law now applied and construed will be the uniform statutory law. The UCCJA is designed to discourage child snatching and end forum shopping (not exactly the same thing), by forbidding courts to legitimize the de facto custody possessed by a parent who has taken a child over a state line or national boundary in violation of another state's previous custody order. It does provide for several exceptions so that this rigid rule will be applied with common sense and in the best interest of children—while seeking to assure that there will not be a whole new exploration and determination of "best interest" every time an interstate dispute comes up.

The UCCJA sets up a number of factors according to which the question of jurisdiction is to be determined, but most of these are fairly decisive ones, which, if conscientiously applied according to the clearly-stated purposes of the Act, will effectively close off any jurisdictional doubts at first glance. It achieves its ends by, primarily, declaring the previously-accepted principle of comity to be the law of the adopting state. It declares its purpose in Section 1, and is so constructed that all judicial decisions under the Act must be designed to achieve the stated purposes. These are the avoidance of jurisdictional competition and conflict between the various state courts, discouraging abductions and re-litigations, and assuring that litigation will take place in the state having the most significant connections with the child.

The Act thus embodies a principle of continuing jurisdiction, recognizing in Sections 12 through 15 that a state which had jurisdiction of a custody matter at one time continues to have it when the parties or the children move. Section 14 declares that, under most circumstances, the state shall not modify a foreign decree. Various provisions make it plain that these principles, which otherwise might hopelessly conflict in a given case, are to be applied in a commonsense way that will not seriously compromise the child's best interest. The Act is not really a reciprocal Act, so a state does not need to have enacted it in order for its citizens to benefit from other states' enactment.

The basic operative section of the UCCJA is Section 3, entitled "Jurisdiction," which sets forth clearly and concisely the principles under which jurisdiction's existence should be determined. Basically, it is the child's home state, or "recent home state" (one that would be the home state if it weren't for a recent abduction) that should determine custody. Thus a state can assume jurisdiction if it is, or has been within six months, the child's home state, and "home state" is to be determined by a "minimum contacts" analysis like that applied in federal constitutional law.

Best interest might dictate jurisdiction in some other state, however. "Best interest" factors that are taken into account include significant connection of the child *and* at least one party with the state, and availability in the state of substantial evidence about the factors that matter in a custody determination. Physical presence is a relevant factor, but the Act makes clear that physical presence alone will not suffice and that presence is not an absolute prerequisite for jurisdiction. Other sections of the Act specifically prohibit entertaining of a lawsuit when there is already a custody determination pending in any other state (Section 6), and require judges to communicate interstate to settle jurisdictional conflicts.

The Act recognizes that two states may have concurrent jurisdiction, and sets forth criteria for when a state should exercise or forbear to exercise the jurisdiction it has. It embodies the principle of forum non conveniens (Section 7) which aids that determination. There is in Section 8 an express adoption of the "clean hands" principle so long known to equity jurisprudence, allowing "jurisdiction to be declined by reason of conduct," but various exceptions are written in to avoid a harsh and unjust effect in particular circumstances.

While surely the spirit of the UCCJA is generally so much in favor of deference to other states' jurisdiction (or recognizing one's own lack of jurisdiction), that any judge could be forgiven for assuming that deference is always a sure way to avoid reversal, there can be reversals for unwarranted refusals to find or exercise jurisdiction. The real mischief that such a refusal can do is explained in *Morgan v. Morgan.* 435 N.Y.S.2d 165, 7 FLR 2203, (N.Y. App. Div. 3d Dept., 1/15/81). It quotes *Nehra v. Uhlar,* 43 N.Y.2d 242, 248, 372 N.E.2d 4, 4 FLR 2120 (N. Y. 1977), to the effect that "no useful purpose on behalf of the child in question is served 'by abstaining from exercise of jurisdiction and thereby projecting another round of protracted and protracting litigation.' "

As noted above, the Act will operate against a background of federal statutory requirement of the same interstate comity result, provided by the new Wallop Amendment to PL 96-611. Enacted in December of 1980, this statute adds Section 1738A to Title 28 U.S. Code to require that states afford full faith and credit to custody decisions and to incorporate Sections 1 through 4 and 12 through 14 of the Act into federal law. It also makes available the IV-D program's Federal Parent Locator Service for interstate custody purposes by adding Section 463 to Title IV-D of the Social Security Act and expresses the intent of Congress that the 18 USC Section 1073 crime of interstate flight extend to cases of children's removal by non-custodial parents. See 7 FLR 1033, 2138. This statute is more fully explained in a separate chapter of this book.

## SOME LIMITATIONS

The Act is not foolproof, since it must have exceptions to avoid draconian effect in human affairs, and it operates mainly as a shield, rather than a sword, in its discouragement of unilateral removals of children. That is, it primarily undertakes to close the courts to those who would legitimatize ill-gotten custody and has considerably less effect on those child-snatchers who are content to stay with their children—even in hiding—without having a document that says they can do so. Thus the Act works best against the worst abuse that inspired its passage—child-snatchers' legitimizing their de facto custody. It is not entirely useless to custodial parents who want to use it more as a sword, however.

One of the most frequently asked questions about the UCCJA is how it can help the custodial parent when the parent who removed the kids is content just to stay with them in a different state, without ever going into court there to seek a custody decree of his own. Actually the Act contemplates more than just passive protection of custody decrees, and has been successfully used for their affirmative interstate enforcement. Sections 16 through 20 of the UCCJA set up a URESA-like procedure for sending on the existing custody decree to the distant state for enforcement there. Of course this practically necessitates the hiring of a lawyer in the distant state, and thus does not fully answer the problem of custodial parents who cannot afford one. However, this Act never purported to solve at a stroke all the problems of indigent parents. Rather, the solution to making return of children more automatic lies in the legislative creation of a system to make out-of-state clients somehow eligible for legal aid.

## OPERATION, REQUIREMENTS AND PROCEDURES GENERALLY

The UCCJA is practically as useful in setting up a rationalized and predictable procedure as it is in declaring jurisdictional policies. However, it will take some time for some courts and counsel to learn it, distracted as they will be by the effort to bend the procedures to a client's own ends in the heat of adversary advocacy. As discussed in detail under "mechanics" below, a court will first determine from the parties' representations and from communication with other states' judges whether it has jurisdiction, and then will determine on the basis of the same evidence, or more if necessary, whether it is appropriate to exercise that jurisdiction. Then and only then will it address the merits of the custody claim.

For the purpose of securing the basic jurisdictional facts from the parties, the UCCJA introduces a procedure which is new in nearly all states: a requirement—which doubtless many judges treat as a jurisdictional requirement—that to get into court at all, both parties supply detailed affidavits as to the child's history and current status.

Several observers have also noted the possibility of constitutional problems in the operation of the Act. Whether a state can adopt comity rules like the UCCJA Sections 12-14 res judicata, recognition, and non-modification provisions is not all that certain. It may just be that constitutionally acceptable personal jurisdiction as the term is used in *Kulko v. California*, 436 U.S. 84, 4 FLR 3075, is necessary to adjudicate a custody issue against a parent. Even before *Kulko*, *Shaffer v. Heitner*, 433 U.S. 186 (1977)—giving no thought whatever to its effect on divisible divorce issues—had all but abolished quasi in rem jurisdiction, and the Court in *May v. Anderson*, 345 U.S. 258 (1953), had rejected the idea that children are merely in rem "incidents" of divorce whose custody can be adjudicated without personal jurisdiction over the affected parent.

# COURT INTERPRETATIONS OF THE UCCJA

## INTERPRETATION GENERALLY

Besides creating a new certainty of expectation about foreign law, the Act also makes available a whole body of interpretive case law from the other states, which lawyers and judges can draw upon. This is in addition to the very clear direction in Section 1 of the Act, concerning "Purposes," which is to guide all application. There are also the explanatory notes compiled by the National Conference of Commissioners on Uniform State Laws, who drafted the Act, and whatever legislative history there may be from a particular state's own legislature.

Certainly the Act is detailed and appears carefully thought out. And yet, there have been a surprising number of these state-court interpretations in recent years, so that on at least a few controversial points an advocate apparently still has some maneuvering room. In fact, if the appellate court opinions are any indication, there is often considerable work for a lawyer to do, no matter which parent is being represented. Probably an advocate will most likely find himself or herself arguing that extraordinary circumstances require the exercise of jurisdiction under the "emergency" exception, disputing "home state" status in the case of a mobile and unsettled family, arguing that other principles outweigh the Section 8 "clean hands" considerations, or arguing the forum non conveniens/best interest question. Battle may rage, and searching debate ensue, over where the equities lie and who it is that UCCJA principles support, when a child-snatching victim has snatched the child back.

## RETROACTIVITY AND ANTICIPATION

Because the Uniform Child Custody Jurisdiction Act is comparatively recent legislation in so many states, arguments over retroactivity do arise, at least as to decisions on custody proceedings filed before the Act's effective date or appeals from pre-Act trial court holdings. For some states it is a simple public policy matter of holding that the salutary principles of the Act deserve retroactive application and that no vested interest accrues from a party's expectation of benefitting by the anarchic conditions the Act seeks to remedy.

Some retroactivity decisions hinge on abstruse principles of individual state constitutional law of little interstate utility, and it is possible in a particular state for the retroactivity question to be governed by the characterization of the Act as substantive or procedural. Though some states in determining retroactivity have gotten hung up on deciding whether the UCCJA's changes are substantive or procedural, finding great difficulty in making this demarcation, the New York court in *Pitrowski v. Pitrowski,* 412 N.Y.S. 2d. 316, 5 FLR 2382 (N.Y. Sup. Ct. Nassau Cty. 1979), and the Montana Supreme Court ruling in *Wenz v. Schwartze,* 598 P. 2d 1086, 5 FLR 2813 at 2814, answered the question by calling the changes procedural in order to accord retroactive effect. The various substantive rules laid down by the Act to give effect to public policy decisions would seem to indicate a substantive character, but in a state which chooses to do without Section 1, which states the Act's purposes, there could be a somewhat stronger argument for calling it strictly procedural. (States that have omitted Section 1 include Florida, Ohio, South Dakota, and Virginia.)

The fact that in most states the Act simply codified what had earlier been recognized as the prevailing and better view has also made retroactive application much easier for some states. The Illinois Appellate Court for the First District resolved the retroactivity question simply by holding that although the Act had not become law when an appealed case arose, "we nevertheless regard the Uniform Act as pertinent to the issues raised and consider them in the light of its policies." (*Weinstein v. Weinstein,* 408 N.E. 2d 952 6 FLR 3075 (1980), citing *Tanner v. Smith,* 378 N.E. 2d 166 (1978), and *Weimer v. Weimer,* 402 N.E. 2d 706, 6 FLR 2437 (1980)).

It is possible, however, for a court to deny retroactive application to a jurisdiction-attaching procedural section of the UCCJA where it would violate arguably vested immunities or rights of due process protection even though the state's highest authority has already opted for application of the Act's salutary substantive principles to pre-Act cases. In *Wilke v. Wilke,* 423 N.Y.S. 2d 249, 6 FLR 2165 (N.Y. App. Div. 2d Dept. 1980), the court refused to apply retroactively the Act's service-by-mail provision. Again it was a New York court that showed similar caution in refraining from a retroactive exercise of the new jurisdictional reach created by UCCJA "recent home state" jurisdiction in *Pitrowski, supra.* It was said there that such a breach of fundamental fairness and legitimate expectations would require a far more explicit statement of legislative intent favoring retroactive application. The North Carolina Supreme Court rejected retroactive application in *Lynch v. Lynch,* 274 S.E. 2d 212, 7 FLR 2277 (1981).

It should be noted that the Act was also retroactively applied in *Wenz v. Schwarze, supra,* and by the Rhode Island Supreme Court majority, over a vigorous dissent, in *Paolino v. Paolino,* 420 A. 2d 830, 6 FLR 2937 (R.I., 1980).

Analyzing problems of retroactivity has been made considerably easier for some states by a related phenomenon perhaps best labeled "anticipation." Comity between states has long been the prevailing rule in custody matters as far as the appellate courts are concerned, and thus such courts as the Washington Supreme Court in *Re Dunkley,* 475 P. 2d 1071, 4 FLR 2305 (1978) (citing a similar action of the Minnesota Supreme Court), expressly applied the principles of the UCCJA while simultaneously recommending that the state legislature adopt it, and explained that its substantive concepts were already the better and prevailing view in Washington State and nationwide. Another example of anticipation is the Minnesota Supreme Court's action in *Re Giblin,* 232 N.W. 2d 214 (1975). New York's highest court was somewhat more cautious in giving the same reason for applying the UCCJA before its effective date but after enactment in *Nehra v. Uhlar,* 372 N.E. 2d 4, 4 FLR 2120 (1977). Similar reasoning was applied by lower New York courts in *Re Shalit,* 4 FLR 2035 (N.Y. Cty. Sup. Ct. 11/1/77); *In re Anonymous,* 395 N.Y.S. 2d 1000, 4 FLR 2199, (N.Y. Cty. Sup. Ct. N.Y. Cty. 1978); *Appelblom v. Appelblom,* 412 N.Y.S. 2d 517, 5 FLR 2250 (N.Y. App. Div. 4th Dept. 1979); and *In re Basil Inn,* 404 N.Y.S. 2d 511, 4 FLR 2504 (N.Y. Fam. Ct. Queens Cty. 1978). Such anticipatory action has been forthrightly taken by the highest court of at least one state that has still not adopted the Act: *Doe v. Roe,* 387 N.E. 2d. 143, 5 FLR 2515 (Mass. 1979), allows those compiling surveys to say that in Massachusetts the UCCJA has been judicially adopted. For another Massachusetts Supreme Judicial Court case applying the UCCJA despite non-enactment see *Murphy v. Murphy,* 404 N.E. 2d. 69, 6 FLR 2517 (1980).

## GROUNDS—HOME STATE

Though there can be numerous reasons under the Act for some state other than the Section 3(2)(1) "home state" to be selected as the proper exerciser of jurisdiction, and numerous cases of "home state versus other ground" are detailed below, it is obvious from the whole scheme and context of the Act that Section 3 sets up a scale of priorities, in which home state jurisdiction is preferred. The Commissioners say as much in their commentary to Section 3 on pages 9 and 10 of their official printing of the Act. They likewise explain there the reason for their choice of six months as the appropriate residence interval: the child's likely integration into the new community by that time. The priority of home state jurisdiction is recognized in *McDonald v. McDonald*, 253 N.W.2d 678, 3 FLR 2540 (Mich. Ct. App. 1978); and *Gaines v. Gaines*, 566 S.W.2d 814, 4 FLR 2487 (Ky. Ct. App. 1978). See also the recognition of priority in *Hegler v. Hegler*, 385 So.2d 1134, 6 FLR 2646 (Fla. Ct. App. 5th Dist. 1980). In *Severn v. Severn*, 608 P.2d 381, 6 FLR 2461 (Colo. Ct. App., 1980) it was held to outweigh the "clean hands" provisions of UCCJA Section 8 that allow jurisdiction to be declined for reasons of parties' conduct. It is a logical reading of the Act that if there is a home state, that state is preferred over other possible possessors of jurisdiction, unless some stated exception applies, and that view was declared by a Florida court in *Hegler*.

At least two states at first statutorily rejected the use of an arbitrary time period for defining the home state. Thus in Kentucky before 1980, the court had to decide in each instance if the interval spent in a given state, under the circumstances, made it the child's home state. See *Freeman v. Freeman*, 547 S.W.2d 437, 3 FLR 2233 (Ky. 1977); and Ky. Rev. Stat. Ann. Section 403.260 (Baldwin Supp. 1977). (See also Ill. Rev. Stat. 1977, ch.40, Sec 601 (2).)

There is some room for lawyerly argument in a UCCJA case over what constitutes "home state" status or sufficient evidence of "significant connection" with a particular state under the basic "jurisdiction" section of the Act, Section 3. Frequently there is a conflict of UCCJA principles, with "home state" being weighed against continuing jurisdiction. Particularly instructive discussions of "home state" are found in *Clark v. Clark*, 416 N.Y.S.2d 330, 5 FLR 2597 (N.Y. App. Div. 3d Dept., 1979), wherein the forum state found that its "recent home state" status was outweighed by continuing jurisdiction considerations favoring the old home state, as well as by "clean hands" considerations, since the child had come to New York by means of a child-snatching.

On the other hand, a Florida appellate court held that the child's recent acquisition of Florida as a "home state" outweighed the Section 8 "clean hands" considerations that would otherwise have required it to defer to an Arizona decree, and its explanation was the traditional one that a court must be prepared to oversee the welfare of a child physically present in its district. *Baird v. Baird*, 374 So. 2d 60, 5 FLR 2812 (Fla. Ct. App. 3d Div., 1979). (It was, however, in that case the custodial parent who removed the child to Florida, and the Arizona decree that was refused deference was one issued in the father's favor by the Arizona courts after mother and child relocated.) For a very broad reading of the home state concept, see *Dykes v. Dykes*, ____So.2d____. 7 FLR 2290 (Fla. Ct. App. 5th Dist. 2/4/81).

Issues of "home state" jurisdiction versus continuing jurisdiction are also discussed in *Palm v. Superior Court*, 158 Cal. Rptr. 786, 5 FLR 2967 (Calif. Ct. App. 4th Div., 1979), which resolved the concurrent jurisdiction situation by deciding that "home state" was outweighed, and in *Policastro v. Policastro*, 5 FLR 2427 (N.Y. Sup. Ct. Suffolk Cty., 2/6/79), in which the acquisition of a new home state by virtue of a 20-month stay after the children's removal by the custodial parent in violation of a New York decree did not bar New York's taking jurisdiction.

Room for controversy is obviously created, even though there should not be more than one home state under Sections 2(5) and 3(a)(1) of the Act, because jurisdiction conferred by home state status can place jurisdiction in a state different from the one given jurisdiction by presence of other jurisdiction grounds under the Act. The obvious one is the continuing jurisdiction created by Sections 12 and 14 ("binding force" and "nonmodification") of the Act. This continuing jurisdiction was held to prevail over home state jurisdiction to produce a fairly harsh result in *Re Bacon*, 412 N.Y. S. 2d 282 (N.Y. Sup. Ct. NY Cty., 1978), wherein New York felt obliged to decline jurisdiction over the case of a child who lived with the mother in New York for nearly all of the time in question—since earlier the mother had nevertheless voluntarily consented to have the case heard in Massachusetts. Having been disappointed by the result there, she was not allowed a second bite in Manhattan.

However, it was held proper for New York to disregard such continuing jurisdiction and modify a previous default custody decree when the Puerto Rico court that rendered it did not any longer have jurisdiction under standards similar to the UCCJA—New York having become the new home state. *Fernandez v. Rodriguez*, 411 N.Y. S. 2d 134 (N.Y. Sup. Ct. Monroe Cty., 1978). The new home state also took jurisdiction in *Settle v. Settle*, 556 P. 2d 962, 3 FLR 2256 (Ore. 1976), wherein an Indiana custody decree never "took effect" and the Oregon family had in fact been gone from Indiana for 18 months. A question of home state versus continuing jurisdiction was resolved in *Howard v. Gish*, 373 A. 2d 1280, 3 FLR 2575 (Md. Ct. Spec. App. 1977) with the declaration that wooden applications of the continuing jurisdiction rule should not take jurisdiction from the home state in which a child has lived virtually all of its life, and should not defeat the intent of the Act to give jurisdiction in the ordinary case to the home state.

The home state status of Illinois, which did not then have the

UCCJA, was honored by California courts in *Re Schwander,* 79 Cal. App. 3d 1013, 145 Cal. Rptr. 325, 4 FLR 2467 (Cal. Ct. App. 2d Dist, 1978), even though the children were in California.

In *Matteson v. Matteson*, 379 So. 2d 677, 6 FLR 2340 (Fla. Ct. App. 2d Dist., 1980) a Florida court explains how New York's home state status and its greater number of significant connections and evidence availability factors outweigh Florida's continuing jurisdiction. A new home state was also deferred to by the continuing jurisdiction state in *Constantino v. Constantino,* 386 So. 2d 1274 (Fla. Ct. App. 3d Dist. 1980). *In re Woods* explains how home state status prevails in determining the appropriate forum in a concurrent jurisdiction situation ((unpublished), 6 FLR 2175 (Calif. Ct. App. 1st Dist., 11/27/79).)

However, other Section 3(a)(2) significant connections were held to outweigh home state status in *Policastro v. Policastro, supra,* and in *Smith v. Superior Court,* 137 Cal. Rptr. 348 (Calif. Ct. App. 1st Dist. 1977). The significant connections that Kentucky had in *Gaines v. Gaines,* 566 S.W.2d 814, 4 FLR 2487 (Ky. Ct. App. 1978) were found insufficient to support jurisdiction when there was a home state somewhere else, and acquisition of a new home state outweighed Kentucky's continuing jurisdiction in *Turley v. Griffin,* 508 S.W.2d 764 (Ky. 1974).

The Illinois Appellate Court for the First District in *Siegel v. Siegel,* 400 N.E.2d 6, 6 FLR 2168 (1979), found that it had continuing jurisdiction to enforce visitation rights by contempt, though it was not the home state anymore, but that was reversed in 1981 (      N.E.2d      , 7 FLR 3009 (Ill. Sup. Ct. 1/20/81)). In *Larsen v. Larsen,* 615 P. 2d 806, 6 FLR 2844 (Kans. Ct. App., 8/15/80), however, continuing jurisdiction and convenience of forum prevailed over new home state. Home state and sufficient connections are found by the court in *Auchincloss v. Kress,* 5 FLR 2966 (N.Y. Sup. Ct. N.Y. Cty., 10/15/79) and recognized in *Re Irene R.,* 5 FLR 2635 (N.Y. Fam. Ct. Westchester Cty., 5/4/79). The need to make an evaluation of home state status before seizing upon other jurisdictional grounds when they are obvious is explained in *Re Donovan R.,* 5 FLR 2845 (Calif. Ct. App. 1st Dist., 7/26/79). *Bergstrom v. Bergstrom,* 271 N.W.2d 540, 5 FLR 3001 (N.D. 1978), made the important point that the residence of which Section 3(a)(1) speaks is actual physical, not "legal" residence.

"Recent home state" jurisdiction, which can exist under Section 3(a)(1)(ii) without the presence of the child within the state, is also discussed in *Gelkop v. Gelkop*, 345 So.2d 195, 6 FLR 2607 (Fla. Ct. App. 3d Dist., 5/28/80); and in *Kern v. Kern*, 87 Cal. App. 3d 402, 50 Cal. Rptr. 860, 5 FLR 2169 (Calif. Ct. App. 1st Dist., 1978). It also received some discussion in *Rexford v. Rexford,* P. 2d , 7 FLR 2205 (Alaska Sup. Ct., 12/26/80). It is the jurisdiction that a state has under Section 3(a)(1)(ii) if it was the child's home state within the last six months, even though the child is now absent from the state, leaving only one parent there. It would obviously apply to a child unconscionably "snatched" away by one parent claiming custody, but it also applies to a child absent for any reason. Obviously this is a short-lived jurisdiction ground which will vanish if a parent does not file quickly. The state might continue to have jurisdiction under other UCCJA sections, however, if it has issued a decree (continuing jurisdiction—or the jurisdiction-like preemptive right that it represents—under Sections 12-14), or if there is Section 3(a)(2)(i) and (ii) "significant connection and evidence-availability" jurisdiction present despite the more-than-six-months' absence, or if no other state would have or will take or exercise jurisdiction (Section 3(a)(4)(i)). (See, however, the Illinois Supreme Court opinion in *Siegel, supra.*) "Recent home state" jurisdiction is found and discussed in *Pitrowski v. Pitrowski,* 412 N.Y.S.2d 316, 5 FLR 2382 (N.Y. Sup Ct. Nassau Cty., 1979).

The importance of home state jurisdiction is demonstrated in *Grubs v. Ross*—a case which makes a great many helpful points. Though it might perhaps be inaccurate to say that the new state's "home state" character outweighed Section 8 "clean hands" considerations and Sections 12-14 continuing jurisdiction considerations, since the father's unilateral removal of his daughter to Oregon was not a classic "child-snatching" situation, and since the original home state's prior decree was issued ex parte after father and child had left the state, it is instructive. The father took the child away with him as soon as the parties separated, and before the mother had filed any kind of suit. Though she got an ex parte custody decree in the meantime, Oregon had been the child's home for three years by the time she tracked the father down in Oregon and sued for custody there. The Oregon trial court properly took jurisdiction, exercised it, and found for the father, the Court of Appeals said (614 P.2d 1225, 6 FLR 2823, (1980)), since Montana no longer had home state or significant connection jurisdiction to be deferred to. Though the father did not violate any court decree or even run out on any pending litigation, the Oregon court treated him as a child-snatcher with unclean hands under Section 8—but still found, notwithstanding, that the clean hands considerations were outweighed. It also noted that the test for modifying any prior custody decree, foreign or domestic, is not "changed circumstances" when that decree was ex parte with no adversary hearing. The Oregon Supreme Court had already emphasized the importance of home state jurisdiction in *Settle v. Settle,* 555 P.2d 962, 3 FLR 2181

(1976), by rewarding an arguably child-snatching mother who took two very small children away from Indiana and managed to keep them away from their father in Oregon for 20 months. Oregon had home state status, significant connections, and the greatest access to relevant evidence, and whatever unclean hands considerations existed were outweighed.

The Indiana Court of Appeals for the First District also held that home state considerations prevailed over the continuing jurisdiction of Indiana when children returned to Indiana. Indiana's continuing jurisdiction, it held, was not sufficient to confer jurisdiction when the children and both parties had since moved away. *Campbell v. Campbell,* 388 N.E. 2d 607, 5 FLR 2616 (1979).

The Rhode Island Supreme Court held that Rhode Island's status as home state at the time a custody modification action seeking some visitation was filed was outweighed by the closer connection that Pennsylvania had by virtue of a wife's moving the kids out of the state after the father filed his action. Though Rhode Island was the home state at the time of filing, the court said, the closer connections of Pennsylvania as the apparently-soon-to-become-home-state, and Massachusetts as the original decree-issuing state, were sufficient to make Rhode Island an inconvenient forum. There was a strong dissent in this case, *Paolino v. Paolino,* 420 A. 2d 830, 6 FLR 2937 (1980). In *Lopez v. District Court,* 606 P. 2d 853, 6 FLR 2308 (1980) the Colorado Supreme Court, rejecting a trial court interpretation, held that home-state status will not outweigh the fact that an action is pending in some other state. Refusal to defer to the decree of a home state that was "improperly acquired" through child-snatching is shown in *Hopson v. Hopson,* 168 Cal. Rptr. 345, 6 FLR 2952 (Calif. Ct. App. 1st Dist., 1980).

The New York Court of Appeals in *Vanneck,* 404 N.E.2d 1278, 6 FLR 2447 (1980), held that for a home state to proceed by enjoining a custody action in the foreign state where the mother has taken the children, and where facts give rise to at least a colorable claim of jurisdiction by the foreign state, does not satisfy the requirements of the UCCJA for the resolution of concurrent-jurisdiction problems. It was held in *Pierce v. Pierce,* 287 N.W. 2d 879, 6 FLR 2399 (Iowa 1980), that a modification of custody was improperly granted in Iowa since Florida had both the home state status and significant connections. Yet it was held in *Wenz v. Schwarze,* 598 P.2d 1086, 5 FLR 2813, 1158 (Mont. 1979), that acquisition of a new home state outweighed continuing jurisdiction elsewhere, because the state that issued the original decree had lost its jurisdiction along with its home state status and its significant connections to the child. The Illinois appellate court in *Weinstein v. Weinstein* went into considerable detail about the strength of connections which can outweigh the home state status of a foreign jurisdiction even when the petitioner filed his custody modification action only a few days after arriving in the forum. After looking to law review articles, case law, and the Commissioners' notes, the court there (408 N.E. 2d 952, 6 FLR 3075 (1980)), held that the significant connections were strong enough to give Illinois a concurrent jurisdiction, and that other factors then dictated deciding the concurrent jurisdiction question in favor of Illinois.

Deciding in favor of custodial grandparents living in a distant state, and against a local natural mother who retained the child after visitation, a Florida court pointed out that the Act nevertheless confers jurisdiction whenever it would be in the child's best interest for the forum to assume it and the forum has significant connections and access to evidence. After saying that, however, the court said the trial court should have declined to exercise the jurisdiction that it had. *Wheeler v. Wheeler*, 383 So. 2d 655, 6 FLR 2478 (Fla. Ct. App. 2d Dist., 1980)

Florida, having long enjoyed a reputation for exercising its jurisdiction when other states would waive it, showed itself getting into the spirit of UCCJA deference in such cases as *Wheeler* and *Hegler*. In the latter the court apparently held that home state jurisdiction outweighs even the continuing jurisdiction of the original decree-issuing state when the children come back to it, and in fact entirely destroys that original-state jurisdiction.

An important point was made by the Maryland Court of Special Appeals in *Paltrow v. Paltrow*, 376 A. 2d 1134, 3 FLR 2716 (1977): that even if a parent defying a prior decree or trying to avoid a pending action has managed to keep the children in the forum for over six months, another state with far stronger connections can be the home state. Whether exactly this way of phrasing the rule might or might not be acceptable to its draftsmen, what the court did there constituted a refusal to let the clock run, and home-state status accrue, when unclean hands and pending foreign proceedings complicated the picture.

## SIGNIFICANT CONNECTION/EVIDENCE AVAILABILITY

Closely related to "home state" is the "significant connection" jurisdiction that a court may have if it is not the Section 3(a)(1) home state or recent home state, but, as specified by Section 3(a)(2), it is in the best interest of the child to assume jurisdiction because the child and at least one litigant have a significant connection with the state *and* substantial evidence relevant to the child's care is available in the forum state. (Thus for example a non-home state might claim "significant connection, etc." jurisdiction if it was the mother's original home and that of her parents, where the children spent several months out of each year, as happened in *Howard v. Howard*, 378 So. 2d 1329, 6 FLR 2241 (Fla. Ct. App. 5th Dist, 1980), and in *Hofer v. Agner*, 373 So. 2d 48 (Fla. Ct. App. 1st Dist., 1979).) This "significant connection" serves as a jurisdiction ground under Section 3, and also is the most obvious component of the decision under Section 7 as to which of two states having jurisdiction shall exercise it. (See Section 7(c)(2).) Often courts find themselves making a rough-hewn balancing evaluation of the *International Shoe v. Washington* (326 U.S. 310 (1945)) sort which resolves it all into a simple matter of perceiving that there is a question of jurisdiction and ruling that jurisdiction goes to the state with the most "significant connections."

One abiding and transcendent problem is that the most significant connections, as well as the child's obvious best interest, may lie in a state where the child came as the result of a child snatching. Some courts, as in *Clark v. Clark*, 404 N.E. 2d 23 (Ind. Ct. App. 1st Dist. 1980), have said that if they must conflict, best interest must prevail over the long range goal of an orderly system of justice, while such cases as *Hopson, supra*, have held otherwise.

In *Policastro v. Policastro*, 5 FLR 2427 (N.Y. Sup. Ct. Suffolk Cty. 2/6/79), as in *Howard* and *Hofer, supra*, it was held that other significant connections outweighed the fact that another state was the child's home state. They also outweighed home-state considerations in *Smith v. Superior Court*, 137 Cal. Rptr. 348, 68 C.A. 3d 457 (Cal. Ct. App. 1st Dist., 1977). A similar result obtained in *Reeve v. Reeve*, 391 So. 2d 789, 7 FLR 2207 (Fla. Ct. App. 1st Dist. 1980), which illustrates how a noncustodial parent can maintain the necessary connections after the child moves away.

A New York court found Section 3 "significant connection" jurisdiction over a child who was in fact in Nigeria, since many factors still connected the family with New York, including the fact that when the father intentionally split the family he left several of the children in New York. *In re Anne A.*, 6 FLR 2876 (N.Y. Fam. Ct. Bronx Cty., 9/10/80).

In *Smith* it was observed that although consent cannot confer jurisdiction, joint submission of the issues to a certain court can be strong evidence of what state the important persons in a child's life consider to be the child's home, and thus can demonstrate the most significant connection. An analysis carefully preserving the distinction between possession and exercise of jurisdiction is found in *Wheeler v.*

*Wheeler,* 383 So. 2d 655, 6 FLR 2478 (Fla. Ct. App. 2d Dist., 1980), which noted that significant connections with the state and presence of evidence there, combined with a determination that it would be in the best interest of a child to assume jurisdiction, can be a ground of jurisdiction—but decided against Florida's exercise of the jurisdiction it thus possessed.

These contests between the significant connection and continuing jurisdiction principles are generally sensitive attempts to strike a proper balance between equally fundamental aims of the UCCJA. It is not always a device invoked by non-home states to rationalize a dubious assumption and exercise of jurisdiction. In *Re Steiner*, 89 Cal. App. 3d 363, 152 Cal. Rptr. 612, 5 FLR 2465 (Cal. Ct. App. 5th Dist., 1979), a foreign holding of Section 3(a)(2) significant connection, best interest and most evidence was deferred to as to a child who by virtue of an unusual alternating custody arrangement stayed less than six months in each state and thus had no "home state."

However, a fairly disturbing tendency of courts to leap at "significant connection" can be discerned in cases such as *Green v. Green,* 276 N.W. 2d 472 (Mich. 1978), and *Nelson v. District Court,* 527 P. 2d 811 (Colo. 1974) (the latter characterized, however, by very unusual facts), which voice the idea that jurisdiction lies when "all persons having an interest in the child's custody" are local residents *or have sought to enforce their rights by petitioning in the forum.*

Many cases focus on what does not amount to significant connection under Section 3 and Section 7. For instance, *Brooks v. Brooks,* 530 P. 2d 547 (Ore. Ct. App. 1975), holds that a state should not defer to the custody-modifying decision of a state where neither parent lived when the action was initiated if the parties' connections with that state were not substantial. Some of the more obvious cases resulting in rejection of significant connection arguments are *McDowell v. Orsini,* 54 Cal. App. 3d 951, 127 Cal. Rptr. 285 (Calif. Ct. App. 2d Dist., 1976); *In re Ben Yehoshua,* 91 Cal. App. 3d 258, 154 Cal. Rptr. 80 (Calif. Ct. App. 5th Dist., 1979); and *Young v. District Court*, 570 P. 2d 249, 4 FLR 2013 (Colo. 1977). Numerous cases construing the "significant connection" provisions, such as *Bacon v. Bacon*, 293 N.W. 2d 819, 6 FLR 2709 (Mich. Ct. App. 1980); *McDonald v. McDonald,* 253 N.W. 2d 678, 4 FLR 2540 (1977); *Neal v. Superior Court,* 148 Cal. Rptr. 841, 5 FLR 2072 (1978), and *Fernandez v. Rodriguez,* 411 N.Y.S. 2d 134, 97 Misc. 2d 353 (N.Y. Fam. Ct. Monroe Cty. 1978), emphasize that, as Section 3 carefully states, mere physical presence of a child in the state is not enough to constitute significant connection. See too *In re Holman,* 396 N.E. 2d 331 (Ill. 1979).

A sage observation on how easy it is to satisfy the Section 3(a)(2) "significant connection" ground of jurisdiction was made in *Wise v. Aldrich*, 6 FLR 2857 (N.Y. Fam. Ct. Rensellaer Cty, 9/2/80), which found it, but nevertheless declined to exercise jurisdiction on forum non conveniens grounds.

Attenuation of the original significant connections that support a state's continuing jurisdiction, so as to justify a new home state's exercising its own jurisdiction, is illustrated in *Wenz v. Schwarze*, 598 P. 2d 1086, 5 FLR 2813 (Mont. 1979). The Minnesota Supreme Court made a particularly insightful distinction when it declared in *Re Mullins*, 298 N.W. 2d 56, 6 FLR 2894 (1980), that "significant connection" does not accrue in a new state as quickly, and the significant connections of the original decreeing state do not attenuate as quickly, when a case involves a third-party foster placement rather than divorced parents.

For cases in which a forum found sufficient "significant connections" to entertain the case despite a parent's having kept the child away long enough to claim a new home state, see *Joseph E.H. v. Jane E.H.*, 423 A. 2d 739, 7 FLR 2119 (Pa. Super. Ct., 1980), and *D.L.S. v. J.L.S.*, 420 A. 2d 625 (Pa. Super. Ct., 1980). These cases, like *Paltrow, supra*, hinged upon the length of the family's pre-separation residence in a state.

## MOST INFORMATION

The "information access" component of this jurisdictional ground is emphasized in other cases. It was emphasized in resolving the concurrent jurisdiction question in *Smith v. Superior Court, supra*, and *Matteson, supra*, in order to decline jurisdiction, and in *Ehr v. Ehr*, 396 N.E. 2d 87, 6 FLR 2127 (Ill. App. Ct. 2d Dist., 1979), and *Settle, supra*, to justify exercising it. In *Ehr* it was considered important that among the evidence available in the forum were reports from doctors and welfare department workers who had examined the child. In *Settle*, it outweighed "clean hands" and continuing jurisdiction considerations raised when a mother took the children to the forum state of Oregon despite a pending Indiana lawsuit. It was an important factor in justifying jurisdiction's exercise in *Brooks v. Brooks, supra*, for the fact that the children were present in the forum and all parties submitted themselves to its jurisdiction guaranteed the maximum information availability. It was cited as the most important factor in *Schlumpf v. Superior Court*, 145 Cal. Rptr. 190, 4 FLR 2448 (Cal. Ct. App. 3d Dist., 1978) by a court declining, in favor of the state where the children were then living, to exercise its valid concurrent jurisdiction.

The "information access" aspect of Section 3(a)(2) was emphasized in *Re Rose M.S.*, 6 FLR 2920, (N.Y. Fam. Ct. Kings Cty., 10/1/80), which served something of a warning on non-custodial parents seeking a custody change. Because the father alleged that the custodial mother's mental state and style of life justified a change in custody, the New York court emphasized their relevance in holding that taking advantage of maximum information availability would dictate deferring exercise of jurisdiction to her state. Information access was held to be sufficient to justify jurisdiction by a non-home state in *Reeve v. Reeve*, 391 So. 2d 789, 7 FLR 2207 (Fla. Ct. App. 1st Dist. 1980), even though the state acknowledged another state had more evidence. Such cases as *Mondy v. Mondy*, So. 2d , 7 FLR 2295 (Fla. Ct. App. 1st Dist., 2/13/81), emphasize the tactical advantage an astute child-snatcher gains by getting a court social worker investigation going immediately upon landing in a state and filing.

## BEST INTEREST

Because "best interest" of the child is a familiar legal standard and one that courts have spent decades learning to exalt over all other rules when custody is involved, it has become a well-worn rut in the path of least resistance. In what is at best a simplistic reading of the jurisdiction-determining Section 3 provisions, lumping together the unequal components of the complicated Section 3 formula under a misleading general label, cases are sometimes decided as though "best interest of the child" were really the ground for assuming jurisdiction in the face of an existing foreign prior decree. These cases are discussed under the exceptions to continuing jurisdiction, below, as though there were a "best interest exception."

## CONTINUING JURISDICTION

Usually, if imprecisely, seen as both a jurisdiction ground and a principle for resolution of concurrent-jurisdiction questions is continuing jurisdiction. The concept is central to the UCCJA scheme of discouraging resort to another state to get a new custody decree superseding an existing one. Since Section 6 discourages simultaneous proceedings by forbidding a court to proceed when jurisdiction has attached already in some other state, and Sections 12 through 14 make prior custody decrees binding and severely limit their modification, a state can be considered to have jurisdiction because it once took jurisdiction and issued a custody decree sometime in the past. It should be added that, strictly speaking, a once-decreeing court does not have jurisdiction unless it would have it anyway under Section 3. (But even so, it could be deferred to under Section 7.) As of this writing it has to be added that often the jurisdiction being "continued" will have been assumed under principles other than those of the UCCJA, since so many states have only recently adopted it and a few are still without the Act.

The UCCJA contemplates that this continuing jurisdiction can be lost—and herein its provisions may be said to partake of some internal inconsistency—by the natural erosion of a child and parent's "significant connection" with the state with the passage of time. Thus many of the litigated UCCJA issues pit continuing jurisdiction principles against the "home state" principle: a dispute in which the parent in a new home state argues that not enough significant connections remain to preserve the continuing jurisdiction that might outweigh home state status. Courts have considerable flexibility here to go whichever way prudence and the child's best interests seem to dictate. Whether continuing jurisdiction can be disregarded in order to effect other UCCJA aims is discussed below under "Loss" and "Exceptions."

That the continuing jurisdiction contemplated by the UCCJA's rule is not absolute is highlighted by the explanation in *Smith v. Superior Court*, 137 Cal. Rptr. 348, 68 C.A. 3d 457 (Cal. Ct. App. 1st Dist., 1977), that the newer and more subtle Uniform Act standard prevails over the old general statute.

Continuing jurisdiction was the rule most states had as to custody decrees long before the Uniform Act (see *Stone v. Stone,* 64 N.E. 86 (Indiana 1902); and *Howard v. Gish*, 373 A. 2d 1280, 3 FLR 2575 (Md. 1977)), but they were more often heard defending their own continuing jurisdiction than deferring to that of other states. Typical examples of deference to continuing jurisdiction, including that accorded by new home states, are found in *Palm v. Superior Court*, 158 Cal. Rptr. 786, 5 FLR 2967 (Cal. Ct. App. 4d Dist., 1979); *Pierce v. Pierce,* 287 N.W. 2d 879, 6 FLR 2399 (Iowa 1980); *Ehr, supra; Carson v. Carson,* 565 P. 2d 763, 4 FLR 2569 (Ore. App. 1977); *Fry v. Ball*, 544 P. 2d 402, 2 FLR 2169 (Colo. 1975); *Brown v. District Court,* 557 P. 2d 384 (Colo. 1976); *Moran v. Moran,* 200 N.W. 2d 263 (N.D. 1972); *Moore v. Moore,* 546 P. 2d 1104, 2 FLR 2525 (Ore. Ct. App. 1976); and *Schlumpf v. Superior Court,* 145 Cal. Rptr. 190, 4 FLR 2448 (Cal. Ct. App. 3d Dist., 1978). The last is a case deferring to continuing jurisdiction of another state even though jurisdiction is recognized to be concurrent. In *Larsen v. Larsen, supra,* Kansas found its own continuing jurisdiction, augmented by convenience of forum, to prevail over the concurrent jurisdiction a new home state possessed.

For its prevalence over home state considerations in a fairly harsh result see *In re Bacon*, 412 N.Y.S. 2d 282, 97 Misc. 2d 688 (N.Y. Sup.

Ct. N.Y. Cty., 1978), wherein the New York court deferred to the decree produced after the custody question had been fully litigated in Massachusetts and decided there in the father's favor, even though the child had lived with her mother in New York for nearly all her life. An exception to the rule was not forthcoming, since the mother had voluntarily chosen to litigate in Massachusetts and presented all her evidence there, and then attacked the Massachusetts decree when she lost.

For cases treating continuing jurisdiction as just one more factor in the "significant connection" calculation, see *Hofer v. Agner, supra, and Joseph E.V. v. Jane E.H., supra.*

## LOSS OF CONTINUING JURISDICTION

It is clear from the wording of Sections 2 and 14 that UCCJA continuing jurisdiction does not last forever, but can be adjudged to have disappeared as a child's significant connections to a state dissipate over time, as described above. Such loss was found in *Detko-Roberts v. Stikelether,* 370 So. 2d 383 (Fla. Ct. App. 4th Dist. 1979); *Hegler v. Hegler,* 383 So. 2d 1134, 6 FLR 2626 (Fla. Ct. App. 5th Dist., 1980); *Constantino v. Constantino,* 386 So. 2d 1274 (Fla. Ct. App. 3d Dist., 1980); and *Matteson v. Matteson,* 379 So. 2d 677, 6 FLR 2340 (Fla. Ct. App. 2d Dist., 1980); and the concept of loss over time reaffirmed in *Honigsberg v. Goad,* 550 S.W. 2d 471, 3 FLR 2227 (Ky. 1976); *Howard v. Gish, supra;* and *Turley v. Griffin,* 508 S.W. 2d 764 (Ky. Ct. App. 1974). See also *Clark v. Superior Court,* 140 Cal. Rptr. 709, 3 FLR 2770 (Cal. Ct. App. 1st Dist. 1977), and *Moore, supra.*

A point about the attenuation of continuing jurisdiction over time with the erosion of the underlying significant connections was made by the Minnesota Supreme Court in *Re Mullins, supra.* It declared that the continuing jurisdiction a court "actively" maintains in a case of the "PINS" or "dependency" sort, which may amount to an overseeing of institutional or foster care placement, is much slower to dissipate than is the "passive" retention of jurisdiction in a divorce-generated custody dispute. Put differently, the same principle is that a child residing in a new state with a divorced parent acquires a "home state" there much faster than a "placed" child would.

## CONCURRENT JURISDICTION

Something not always appreciated by those not yet familiar with the Uniform Child Custody Jurisdiction Act is that it definitely contemplates two or more states' possibly having concurrent jurisdiction—a situation rendered more palatable by the Act's all-pervasive recognition of a distinction between having jurisdiction and exercising it. Cases which recognize this concurrent jurisdiction, but show how resourcefully parent-litigants who are willing to travel will try to exploit it, include *Verbin v. Verbin*, 595 P. 2d 905, 5 FLR 2636, (Wash. 1979); and *Carson v. Carson*, 579 P. 2d 846, 4 FLR 2569 (Ore. 1978). On the other hand, *Mort v. Mort*, 365 So. 2d, 194, 5 FLR 2325 (Fla. Ct. App. 4th Dist. 1978) explains that concurrent jurisdiction does not mean concurrent exercise, and holds that a Florida court improperly stayed Florida custody proceedings to give a child-snatching mother time to institute proceedings in Pennsylvania. *Mort* stresses that jurisdiction can never be *exercised* by two states at once under the UCCJA. *Schlumpf v. Superior Court*, 145 Cal. Rptr. 190, 4 FLR 2449 (Calif. Ct. App. 3d Dist., 1978) emphasizes the ability of jurisdiction to exist in two states at once, as it holds that California, having jurisdiction, should have stayed its exercise in the case's particular circumstances. *Allison v. Superior Court*, 99 Cal. App. 3d 993, 160 Cal. Rptr. 309 (Cal. Ct. App. 2d Dist., 1979), explains concurrent jurisdiction. (For a theory, unaccepted so far by Commissioners or courts, that no concurrent jurisdiction exists, see 14 Fam. L.Q. 203 (1981).)

## THE EXERCISE DECISION

Once it has been found that two states have jurisdiction concurrently the question of which state should exercise its jurisdiction is to be resolved in accordance with the Section 1 Purposes of the Act by looking to three things: priority of filing (Section 6), forum non conveniens (Section 7), and the "clean hands" provisions of Section 8. Since Section 6 is mandatory for the state of later filing, but not for the state of first filing, the decision will not necessarily be made by the state where the litigation started first. No state is allowed to proceed if an action still pending was first filed elsewhere unless that state waives its higher right to proceed, but it may well do that if the judges communicate as they are required to do under Section 6. The decision they make there should be controlled by Section 7 and Section 8 considerations. Thus the ugly effects of statutorily encouraging a race to the court house—something the mandatory language of Section 6 clearly does—are somewhat tempered.

Ways of deciding the "exercise" question in a concurrent jurisdiction situation are spread throughout the Act. The basic Section 3 on jurisdiction contemplates ascertaining whether a court having jurisdiction has declined to act (Section 3(a)(4)). Section 6 forbids proceeding simultaneously and requires judges to communicate interstate to avoid it, Section 8 allows a state having jurisdiction to decline its exercise in order to discourage forum-shopping conduct, and most importantly,

Section 7 sets up forum non conveniens as the question to be determined and the ground on which a state having jurisdiction should properly decline.

To facilitate the requirements of Section 6 as well as Section 7, Section 9 of the Act requires litigants to submit under oath any information they may have about proceedings pending elsewhere. Several recent cases have concerned this requirement. They are discussed under "Mechanics" below.

## PENDING CASES

It is an important aspect of the UCCJA's continuing jurisdiction rule that a court acquires its continuing jurisdiction upon the mere initiation of a case, even though no decree exists to be honored at that time. The mandatory language of Section 6, "Simultaneous Proceedings in Other States," bars a court from exercising its jurisdiction if at the time the petition was filed therein, a custody case concerning this child was pending in any other state. It is in this situation that, as Section 6 contemplates, the two judges will actually communicate by mail or telephone to work out the awkward situation with a mutually satisfactory decision as to appropriate forum. However, it has been noted that if the judges fail in their obligation to communicate—whether by unlawful failure of a party parent to disclose the pendency of foreign proceedings as required of him or her by Section 9 or for whatever other reason—the mandatory language of Section 6(a) is left to operate by itself and strict priority of filing must control. See *Weinstein v. Weinstein, supra.* That the Section 6(a) requirement of deference to another state's pending proceedings is absolutely mandatory is a point often made by appellate courts, as in *Bacon v. Bacon,* 293 N.W. 2d 819, 6 FLR 2709 (Mich. Ct. App. 1980); *De Passe v. De Passe,* 421 N.Y.S. 2d 497, 6 FLR 2108 (N.Y. App. Div. 4th Dept., 1979); *Vanneck v. Vanneck,* 417 N.Y.S. 2d 258, affirmed 404 N.E. 2d 1278, 6 FLR 2447 (N.Y. Ct. App., 1980); *Bergstrom v. Bergstrom,* 271 N.W. 2d 540, 5 FLR 3001 (N.D. 1978); *In re Rector,* 565 P. 2d 950 (Colo. Ct. App., 1977); *Barcus v. Barcus,* 278 N.W. 2d 646, 5 FLR 2634 (Iowa 1979); *Palm v. Superior Court*, 158 Cal. Rptr. 786, 5 FLR 2967 (Calif. Ct. App. 4th Dist., 1979); indicating that it is a point which often needs to be made to trial courts. The California court in *Hopson, supra,* declared that violation of this deference requirement is an excuse for refusing to accord continuing jurisdiction effect, or non-modifiability, to any decree that results.

Yet prompt as this "automatic" deference ought to be, there can be a defect in a pending foreign exercise of jurisdiction, just as there can be in a completed one, and perhaps courts have a duty at least to investigate such questions as whether that pending exercise is of a jurisdiction assumed "under principles similar to those of the Act." For an example see *Hanson v. Hanson,* 379 So. 2d 967 (Fla. Ct. App. 1st Dist., 1979) and the comments thereon of Melvyn Frumkes in the Florida State Bar CLE outline on the UCCJA in "Support, Custody and Marital Property in Florida" (1981) p. xxiii. See also *Weinstein, supra, Hopson, supra,* and *Pasqualone, supra.*

The deference required to be afforded to a jurisdiction that is just being (or about to be) assessed in a pending custody suit, and if found exercised, is part of the continuing jurisdiction principle. However, it is discussed here under a separate heading. It could be said by virtue of Section 6 on avoidance of "simultaneous proceedings" that "continuing jurisdiction" is something which attaches upon the mere filing of a suit. However, it would appear more useful to confine the phrase "continuing jurisdiction" to that jurisdiction which continues after a state's courts have heard and passed on the custody of a particular child, and to regard the avoidance of simultaneous proceedings by required deference to pending exercises of jurisdiction as a different phenomenon.

In fact, in courts' consideration of the continuing jurisdiction principle, an important distinction is occasionally drawn between that full adversary determination of the jurisdictional and substantive custody questions that the Uniform Act contemplates and something less: the default and other ex parte determinations so common in interstate cases. These include the judgments that issue upon defective notice, the so-called "punitive decrees" that issue without any exploration of the child's welfare, etc. These are discussed under "exceptions" below.

Examples of deference to pending jurisdiction despite other considerations *contra* include *Palm v. Superior Court, supra*; *In re Pierce,* 601 P. 2d 1179, 6 FLR 2028 (Mont., 1979), *Schlumpf, supra,* and the cases cited therein, and the fairly harsh result in *Re Bacon, supra.* An example of continuing-jurisdiction effect being extended to a mere separation agreement is the New York Court of Appeals' 1979 decision in *Re Corradino,* 400 N.E. 2d 1338, 6 FLR 2204. The Colorado Supreme Court in *Lopez v. District Court,* 606 P. 2d 853, 6 FLR 2308 (1980), provided an interpretation of the Section 6 "simultaneous litigation avoidance" provision that will be useful to some racers to the court house when it held that a case is "pending" for Section 6 purposes from the moment it is filed, rather than the time that actual notice is effected by service of process.

The exercise of local jurisdiction was held precluded by pending foreign proceedings in *Bergstrom, Paltrow, McDonald, Bosse, Rector,* and *Appelblom,* all *supra.* The "pending case" bar was less effective in *Williams v. Zacher,* 581 P. 2d 91, 4 FLR 2674 (Ore. Ct. App. 1978), where it was held that Colorado (a UCCJA state) was not exercising jurisdiction under rules "substantially in conformity" to the UCCJA when it acted after insufficient notice and none of the parties lived there. Nor did the "pending" objection prevail in *Re Steiner*, 89 Cal. App. 3d 363, 152 Cal. Rptr. 612 (Calif. Ct. App. 5th Dist. 1979) which held that a foreign court's order was valid and had to be deferred to, since the local trial court's standard retention of jurisdiction over all custody cases was not tantamount to "pendency." The strict rule of Section 6 was ignored without excuse according to the dissent in *Mondy v. Mondy, supra.* The rather unremarkable holding that a case is not "pending" for UCCJA purposes once it has concluded can be found in *Wheeler v. District Court*, 526 P. 2d 658, 1 FLR 2007 (Colo. 1974), and in *Carson v. Carson,* 579 P. 2d 846, 4 FLR 2569 (Ore. Ct. App. 1977).

## FORUM NON CONVENIENS

The next determination to be made after a court finds it has jurisdiction is whether to exercise it or defer to some other state having jurisdiction (or even, in unusual cases, to one lacking jurisdiction under standards like the Act's—as explained by the Commissioners' commentary to Section 6). Although these principles include more than the forum non conveniens which is mentioned as a justification of non-exercise in Section 7 of the Act, forum non conveniens is valid shorthand for the entire discretionary decision on whether to exercise jurisdiction or decline to. The Section represents an important change in the law for any state—and there is at least one—in which forum non conveniens was never a part of the state law and the idea has grown up that if jurisdiction exists, a court must exercise it. The Section lists a number of factors that may determine the question of a forum's appropriateness—home state, significant connection, evidence-availability, possible agreement by the parties on a forum—and the last of them is whether exercise of jurisdiction would contravene the purposes of the Act. When the court in *Schlumpf, supra,* applied Section 7 on forum non conveniens it employed the home state, significant connection, and most-information factors, for instance, and decided that Colorado should be deferred to. Some factors that trigger the forum non conveniens determination are set out in *Williams v. Zacher,* 581 P.2d 91, 4 FLR 2674 (Ore. Ct. App. 1978). *Williams* also illustrates the relativity of it: the court there said, in effect, "We may be inconvenient, but all other states are more so."

The effect of forum non conveniens thinking is illustrated by *Wheeler v. Wheeler, supra*, in which the Court of Appeal for the Second District of Florida, a state which has historically been unusually ready to accept jurisdiction after child-snatchings, points out that a trial court's having jurisdiction did not oblige it to exercise it. Honoring the Tennessee custody decision that gave a child to its grandparents, the appellate court decided the case against the Florida natural mother who kept her own children after the visitation period.

*Wenz v. Schwartze,* 598 P.2d 1089, 5 FLR 2138 (Mont. 1979), explains the mechanics of the decision-making process that leads to determining forum non conveniens, and emphasizes that the decision to defer on that ground is entirely discretionary. On the other hand, *Mort v. Mort,* 365 So.2d 194, 5 FLR 2325 (Fla. Ct. App. 4th Dist., 1978) appears to lay down a rule that a state which has jurisdiction, yet defers to another state in which there is *no* Section 6 pending determination, must have first held itself an incovenient forum. This is closer to the old view apparently prevailing in a few states before the UCCJA that any state having jurisdiction must exercise it. Somewhat similar in its implications is *Webb v. Webb,* 266 S.E.2d 463, 6 FLR 2448 (Ga. Sup. Ct. 1980), holding that a state can take as well as give up jurisdiction by making a forum non conveniens finding, even if it means accepting jurisdiction despite pending litigation in another state. (Review of this case on certiorari was granted October 6, 1980 —not on a question of UCCJA interpretation, of course, but on the question whether the Full Faith and Credit Clause should apply to custody decisions. No. 79-6853, see 6 FLR 2945, 7 FLR 2353).

For cases finding the forum inconvenient, see *Winkleman v. Moses,* 279 N.W.2d 897, 5 FLR 2709 (S.D. 1979), *Moore v. Moore,* 546 P.2d 1104, 2 FLR 2525 (Ore. Ct. App. 1976); and *Mayer v. Mayer,* 283 N.W.2d 591, 5 FLR 2748 (Wisc. Ct. App. 1979), which found an abuse of discretion in not considering the forum non conveniens factors. For a refusal to defer exercise of jurisdiction after considering the Section 7 factors, see *Breneman v. Breneman,* 284 N.W.2d 804, 6 FLR 2074 (Mich. Ct. App. 1979), which emphasizes the discretionary character of the decision to be made, and *Etter v. Etter,* 405 A.2d 760, 5 FLR 2944 (Md. Ct. Spec. App. 1979). The discretionary character of Section 7 is also emphasized in *Larsen v. Larsen, supra*, which reviews a number of cases on the point. However, a California case, *Hopson, supra,* declares that deference to the convenient forum once a forum finds itself less convenient is absolutely mandatory. It cites *Carson v. Carson, supra,* for this proposition.

For international application of the forum non conveniens doctrine see *Taylor v. Taylor,* Pa. Super. Ct. Phila. Dist. (No. 251, October term 1978, 5/30/80).

A case such as *Clark v. Clark, supra,* serves as a reminder that despite the universally accepted doctrine that jurisdiction cannot be conferred by consent, the parties' agreement can, under Section 7(c) (4), determine the question of convenient forum. In cases where both parties appear the resolution of the Section 7 question is not necessarily predictable. In a trial court decision, *Wise v. Aldrich,* 6 FLR 2857 (N.Y. Fam. Ct. Rens. Cty., 9/2/80), the out-of-state wife appeared, perhaps specially, to argue the question of forum non conveniens and the trial judge decided it in her favor (providing at the same time a good example of how the decision should properly be approached, and a useful practical formula for implementation of the decision to defer). But in *Re Weinstein,* 408 N.E.2d 952, 6 FLR 3075 (Ill. App. Ct. 1st Dist., 1980), after both parties appeared and presented evidence and the decision had been reached, the court on appeal was able to tell the disappointed party who argued inconvenient forum that forum non conveniens considerations are of little weight in attacking a custody decision founded upon personal appearance of both parties and their witnesses and full inquiry by the local trial court. The same thing happened in *Lustig v. Lustig* 299 N.W.2d 375, 7 FLR 2195 (Mich Ct. App. 1980). *Vanneck v. Vanneck,* 417 N.Y.S.2d 258, 404 N.E.2d 1278, 6 FLR 2447 (N.Y. 1980), makes it clear that it is not a forum non conveniens decision, or even a discretionary one, that the court is to make when a case is pending in another state as contemplated by Section 6 on simultaneous proceedings and their avoidance.

The New York Family Court for Bronx County decided in *Re Anne A.,* 6 FLR 2876 (9/10/80), that one who unilaterally removes the children from the forum state (even if it is before the filing of any action) cannot argue forum non conveniens. A majority of the Rhode Island Supreme Court came up with some unusual reasons for a home state to find forum non conveniens when it decided that it was wrong for a trial court to continue to entertain the visitation petition that a non-custodial Massachusetts father filed in Rhode Island back when Rhode Island was the mother and children's home state. Since the mother had moved to Pennsylvania after he filed the petition, the court said, and had told the court she had intended to reside permanently in Pennsylvania, Pennsylvania would have closer connections to the family and this would be decisive of the Section 7 forum non conveniens issue. The dissenter pointed out that this policy, placing a premium on removals of children for jurisdiction-shopping purposes, could keep litigation going indefinitely, once it occurs to a mother that all she need do is move after the husband files in order to force him to start the litigation process all over again. *Paolino v. Paolino, supra.*

Forum non conveniens was found, and jurisdiction's exercise thus declined, in *McDonald v. McDonald, supra; Bosse, supra; In re Anonymous, supra; Carson, supra; Paltrow v. Paltrow,* 376 A.2d 1134, 3 FLR 2716 (Md. Ct. Spec. App. 1977); *Kern v. Kern,* 150 Cal. Rptr. 860, 5 FLR 2169 (Calif. Ct. App. 1st Dist. 1978); and *Gross v. Kellerman,* 404 N.Y.S.2d 178 (N.Y. App. Div. 4th Dept., 1978).

An Alaska case serves as a reminder that a state can defer under Section 7 to a state having no jurisdiction. It also serves as a reminder that Section 7, and the eagerness of some states to defer jurisdiction's exercise, can be taken advantage of by resourceful counsel intent on defeating the aims and spirits of the Act. A mother had arrived in California and immediately filed. Because the California court promptly started up a custody investigation, compiling psychiatric reports, etc., it was held by the Alaska Supreme Court in *Rexford, supra,* that the "most information" principle weighed in favor of California so as to make it a convenient forum. (At the same time the court emphasizes that to give weight to the mere passage of time after a child-snatching is to defeat the ends of the UCCJA, and that cooperation with custody investigators from the new state does not give it jurisdiction or waive the recent home state's jurisdiction. Moving swiftly for an investigation is what makes the difference.)

For Section 7 significance of parties' respective finances, see *Allison v. Superior Court,* 99 Cal. App. 3d 993, 160 Cal. Rptr. 309 (Cal. Ct. App. 2d Dist. 1979).

## CLEAN HANDS

Another ground on which jurisdiction, though possessed, can be "non-exercised" if a court in its discretion be so advised, is the "clean hands" provision of the Act, Section 8 on "jurisdiction declined by reason of (parties') conduct." There are two discretionary situations and one mandatory one. Section 8(a) says the court "may decline" to exercise jurisdiction for a petitioner for *an initial decree* who has wrongfully taken a child from another state or engaged in similar conduct—while Subsection (b) says the court "shall not" exercise its jurisdiction to modify *an existing decree* after improper removal of the child from its custodian "unless required in the interest of the child." The Commissioners' notes explain that as to pre-decree unilateral removals of a child, what is "wrongful" is determined not as a matter of legal rights (which, they admit, would mean no wrongfulness in pre-decree removals), but by considering whether one party's "conduct is so objectionable that a court . . . cannot in good conscience permit that party access to its jurisdiction." The deeper philosophical question over which the Commissioners tread so lightly—whether the two are indeed so separable that there can be a wrong without a right—may someday have to be faced and resolved. Until then, this rough and ready use of definitions serves as a practical expedient.

As for the mandatory Subsection (b), the Commissioners emphasize that "refusal of jurisdiction is mandatory unless the harm done to the child by a denial of jurisdiction outweighs the parental misconduct." Their gloss on the word "improperly" explains how it was added to exclude cases wherein the child was withheld from the lawful custodian because of illness, emergency, or other special circumstances.

Subsection (b), it should be noted, also addresses itself to the wrongfulness of "other violations of custody decrees." The Commissioners' notes make plain that by this addition they are recognizing as raising a serious legal issue the removal of a child from a state by the custodial parent, destroying the other parent's visitation rights. Here, however, it sets up an entirely *discretionary* refusal to extend jurisdiction for decree modification.

It should be noted that the section also includes what the Commissioners call a "financial deterrent": charging the petitioner with fees and expenses of the other party upon dismissing a petition. The financial losses in child-snatching, which Section 8(c) provisions attempt to alleviate, are emphasized by the opinions in *Schwander* and *Mitchell v. Pincock, supra.*

The crucial distinctions between the rules governing Section 8(a) cases, and the two different species of Section 8(b) cases, as well as the extent to which complex equitable considerations can become tangled, are emphasized in the bitterly divided Pennsylvania Supreme Court's three-opinion decision in *Zaubi v. Zaubi,* 423 A2d 333, 7 FLR 2055 (1980, affirming 6 FLR 2306). The majority rejects the idea that in speaking only of a "petitioner" having unclean hands Section 8 precludes refusal to entertain a defendant child-snatcher's defenses when a foreign parent sues to enforce.

The "clean hands" section has been discussed by the courts in such cases as *Barcus v. Barcus,* 278 N.W.2d 646, 5 FLR 2634 (Iowa 1979); *Weimer v. Weimer,* 402 N.E.2d 706, 6 FLR 2437 (Ill. App. Ct. 1st Dist. 1980); *Nehra v. Uhlar,* 43 N.Y. 2d 242, 372 N.E. 2d 4, 4 FLR 2120 (N.Y. 1977); *In re Shalit,* 4 FLR 2035 (N.Y. Sup. Ct. N.Y. Cty., 11/1/77); *Van Heren v. Van Heren,* 407 A.2d 1242, 6 FLR 2075 (N.J.A.D. 1979); *Clark v. Clark,* 416 N.E.2d 330, 5 FLR 2597 (N.Y.A.D. 3d Dist. 1979); *In re Schwander,* 79 Cal. 3d 1013, 145 Cal. Rptr. 325, 4 FLR 2467 (1978); *Williams v. Zacher,* 581 P.2d 91, 4 FLR 2674 (Ore. Ct. App. 1978); *Neal v. Superior Court,* 148 Cal. Rptr. 841, 5 FLR 2072 (Calif. Ct. App. 2d Dist. 1978); *McDonald v. McDonald,* 253 N.E.2d 678, 3 FLR 2540 (Mich. Ct. App. 1977), and *Mitchell v. Pincock,* 577 P.2d 343, 4 FLR 2336 (Id. 1978).

Of course this basic expresssion of the whole UCCJA idea of not rewarding child snatching and forum shopping was the law in many states long before the Uniform Act. See *In re Forsythe*, 546 P.2d 117, 2 FLR 2484 (Wash. Ct. App. 1976); *Perrenoud v. Perrenoud*, 480 P.2d 749 (Kans. 1971); *Fahrinbruch v. People*, 453 P.2d 601 (Colo. 1969); *Clampitt v. Johnson*, 359 P.2d 588 (Okla. 1961); *Ex parte Wenman*, 165 P.2d 1024 (Calif. Ct. App. 1917). And in fact, it is not always certain in those cases such as *Weimer* and *Nehra*, which have produced a retroactive application of the "clean hands" provision, whether it was truly retroactive application, or application of the similar pre-Act policy to a case that arose before the Act took effect.

The fact that a pre-litigation unilateral removal of the child triggers only the discretionary clean hands provision of UCCJA Section 8(a) is emphasized in *Mondy, supra*, and by *Grubs v. Ross*, a case in which the forum's becoming a child's new home state after such a "snatching", if it can be called that, outweighed Section 8 considerations. It was thus held proper for an Oregon court to refuse to defer to Montana jurisdiction. The fact that the mother secured an ex parte decree by litigation started after the father and daughter left the state was held not to change this, since such decrees are not the sort of court orders for such the UCCJA demands respect. Similarly, in *McDonald v. McDonald, supra*, although the court's reason was not articulated in Section 8 terms, the court recognized the impropriety of the mother's pre-litigation unilateral removal of the child but refused to honor the ex parte temporary custody order that the ex-husband secured in Washington state after the mother and daughter surreptitiously left—the ground being that (as the Commissioners' Notes to Section 8 acknowledge) a child's custody should not be used to reward virtue or punish guilt. It did this while simultaneously telling the mother who had brought the child to Michigan that her case could not qualify for jurisdiction in the Michigan courts. It thus—apparently—left the custody matter in limbo while refusing to entertain the case or enforce the foreign order.

Misuse of Section 8 against a party who arguably child-snatched, but is not seeking to forum-shop, was curbed in *Parks v. Parks*, 7 FLR 2274 (Pa. Super. Ct., 2/13/81).

An unwarranted extension of Section 8's meaning was rejected by the Florida Court of Appeal for the First District in *Jennings v. Jennings*, 392 So.2d 352, 7 FLR 2204 (1980). That was a novel theory that violation of some terms of a detailed temporary custody order—taken into account in the initial decision on a final order—should disqualify a distant state from jurisdiction over a case when a parent moves years later for a custody modification. The 1976 Idaho decree recited that after a temporary custody order giving him visitation rights, the father took the boys out of state during his visitation period, and let them stay overnight in the home of a homosexual. Since this conduct was taken into account by the Idaho court in making the original decree, the Florida appellate court said, it had no effect on the present Florida jurisdiction question. Section 8 simply does not apply to improper conduct of a present petitioner for modification which took place before the entry of the custody decree he now seeks to modify. It certainly does not apply when the court making the original decree took the conduct into account and the offender has already been punished once. It would be ridiculous, the court indicated, to hold that a parent is forever foreclosed from suing to modify a foreign custody decree even when there has been a change of circumstances and the parent's life has been circumspect for years.

Other cases illustrate how unclean hands considerations can cancel each other out when considered by a court of equity looking perspicaciously at all the equities. *In Williams v. Zacher*, the moral equities were considered as balancing one another out, clearing the way for a decision that home state status outweighed even the "pending" considerations of Section 6. The court apparently avoided the question whether the child's removal in that case constituted an "initial decree" situation under Section 8(a) or something involving more serious misconduct. It also held that the fact that litigation is pending elsewhere is insignificant if the foreign state is not exercising jurisdiction substantially in conformity with the Act. Also, in *Van Heren, supra*, the court refused to apply Section 8 "clean hands" principles for the benefit of a child snatcher when the spouse snatched the child back. *Bosse v. Superior Court*, 152 Cal. Rptr. 665, 5 FLR 2501 (Calif. Ct. App. 1st Dist. 1979), holds that the best interest of the child, at least where it favors deferring to a sister state, outweighs "clean hands" considerations.

The fact that clean hands considerations are relative was also emphasized by *Nelson v. District Court*, 527 P.2d 811, 814 (Colo. 1974). There it was held that a mother's refusing to permit return of the child to her "legal custodian" (a named but otherwise unidentified woman) in another state does not always preclude Colorado's courts from hearing the case. This was a case in which the child's mother kept her in Colorado in order to litigate, and both parties had significant connections with Colorado, as did the child, even though the child was domiciled in Montana. It was held that when the best interest of the child requires that Colorado exercise jurisdiction, "clean hands" considerations are overriden. In support the court cited *Kennedy v. Carman*, 471 S.W.2d 275 (Miss. Ct. App. 1971); and *Hawkins v. Hawkins*, 504 P.2d 709 (Ore. 1972).

The New York Family Court, Bronx County, in *Re Anne A.*, 6 FLR

2876 (9/10/80), emphasized clean hands considerations in holding that one who unilaterally removes children from the foreign state—even before the divorce—cannot argue forum non conveniens. The New York Supreme Court for Queens County illustrated in *Gomez v. Gomez*, 6 FLR 2903 (9/19/80), how unclean hands considerations can balance one another out, as it exercised jurisdiction at the behest of a child-snatching father who violated an original decree that was granted without hearing by a state having no significant connections with the children at the time of the decree or at any later time.

Other cases in which unclean hands were found include *In re Anonymous, supra; Bacon, supra;* and *In re Potter*, 377 N.E.2d 536 (Ohio 1978). They were alleged but not found in *Bosse, supra,* and *Fernandez v. Rodriguez*, supra. Cases in which jurisdiction was exercised despite the presence of Section 8 considerations include *Williams v. Zacher, supra; Settle, supra;* and *Nehra v. Uhlar, supra.*

Clean hands considerations were emphasized in *Bias v. Bias*, 374 So.2d 64 (Fla. Ct. App. 3d Dist. 1979), a case roundly criticized by Melvyn Frumkes in his Florida State Bar CLE presentation, *supra*, for refusal to acknowledge dissipation of the original significant connections supporting continuing Florida jurisdiction. The court in *Hopson v. Hopson*, 6 FLR 2952 (Cal. Ct. App. 1st Dist., 10/6/80) declared that a child's asking to be removed by the non-custodial parent to another state does not make Section 8 inapplicable.

## MECHANICS

Sometimes questions arise as to UCCJA procedures as courts attempt to mesh its devices with the kinds of procedures and remedies they had become used to. Sometimes trial courts fix on a particular provision of the UCCJA as one which authorizes a quick decision, and do not follow the careful procedures, requiring at least two determinations, which the Commissioners who drafted the Act had in mind. Opinions which explain the two-tier determination of jurisdiction and appropriateness of jurisdiction's exercise that a court should go through include *Wenz v. Schwartze*, 598 P.2d 1086, 5 FLR 2813 (Mont. 1979); *Clark v. Clark*, 404 N.E. 2d 23 (Ind. Ct. App. 1st Dist. 1980); *Campbell v. Campbell*, 388 N.E. 2d 607, 5 FLR 2616 (Ind. Ct. App. 1st Dist. 1979); *Carson v. Carson*, 565 P.2d 763, 4 FLR 2569 (Ore. Ct. App. 1977); and *Etter v. Etter*, 405 A. 2d 760, 5 FLR 2944 (Md. Ct. App. 1979).

Cases which emphasize the sometimes-neglected point that the UCCJA requires trial courts to make a specific express finding on the jurisdiction issue before proceeding to the substantive issue of custody include *Clark v. Clark, supra; In re Donovan R.*, 5 FLR 2845 (Cal. Ct. App. 1st Dist. 7/26/79); *Campbell, supra; Settle v. Settle,* 550 P.2d 445 (Ore. Ct. App. 1976, reversed on other grounds, 556 P.2d 962, 3 FLR 2181); *Clark v. Superior Court,* 73 Cal. App. 3d 300, 140 Cal. Rptr. 709, 3 FLR 2270 (Cal. Ct. App. 1st Dist. 1977); *Bosse v. Superior Court,* 152 Cal. Rptr. 665, 5 FLR 2501 (Cal. Ct. App. 1st Dist. 1979); and *Ehr v. Ehr,* 396 N.E. 2d 87, 6 FLR 2127 (Ind. Ct. App. 2d Dist. 1979).

The view of the appellate courts which insist on a mandatory double-finding procedure may be a dangerously impractical one. Given the vastly overcrowded dockets of most family courts, and given the tremendously increased popularity of divorce in these times, most family court judges are practical men and women seeking to dispense justice without the expediture of any unnecessary court time. However, the finding of jurisdiction can be a very time-consuming but unnecessary step in a case wherein the court is certain that it would decline to exercise any jurisdiction it might possess. For instance, the question whether a given state in which a child-snatcher resorts to the courts for legitimation of his act might possibly have some Section 3(a)(2) jurisdiction to share with the home state could challenge the wisdom of Solomon in many all-too-common cases. But if the child-snatcher could show nothing but Section 3(a)(2) facts and the home state status of the other jurisdiction was clear, the policy considerations of Section 1, Section 7 and Section 8 would probably leave the court with little doubt of what it should do. But the finding of the purely academic question whether this non-home-state forum possesses jurisdiction could take an inordinate amount of researching and decision-making time at a point when swift disposition of the case is crucial to the welfare of the child and a long line of other litigants with cases equally crucial to children's welfare is waiting on the docket and outside the courtroom door.

Counsel should also be prepared to argue, under whatever esoteric state-law doctrines obtain, an abstract question of whether UCCJA adoption wipes out habeas corpus as a custody-litigation vehicle in interstate, and even intrastate, cases, and whether it matters. Though the filing of certified copies of a prior custody decree in a UCCJA Section 15 case is permissive rather than mandatory, courts mistakenly treating it as mandatory can be referred to *Baird v. Baird,* 374 So.2d 60 (Fla. Ct. App. 3d Dist. 1979).

Cases condemning parties' failure to comply with the Section 9 duty to supply information on other proceedings include the Indiana opinion in *Clark, supra,* and *Pasqualone v. Pasqualone,* 406 N.E. 2d 1121,

6 FLR 2744 (Ohio Sup. Ct., 1980). In *Pasqualone*, these mandatory disclosure requirements were rather unusually applied, the court apparently taking the view that one parent's non-compliance with them took the case entirely outside the UCCJA sphere and thus required the case to be decided under federal constitutional law. In *Weinstein v. Weinstein, supra* (the case in which the Illinois Appellate Court for the First District decided (6/24/80) that a concurrent jurisdiction issue should be resolved, absent court communication and agreement, by strict priority of filing date), the court held that non-compliance with these declaration requirements can constitute "unclean hands" under Section 8, and held that the equities do not favor a mother who obtained custody in a foreign proceeding without informing the foreign court that an Illinois action had already been filed. The court in fact could not really be sure the mother had not told the foreign court about the Illinois proceeding, but it held her responsible for not establishing as a matter of record that she so informed it.

Because nothing in the language of Section 9, which embodies this affidavit requirement, seems to limit its application to interstate cases, it has been noticed by judges and practitioners in several states that these affidavits could be demanded in all custody cases, whether they have an interstate aspect or not. Though doubtless this time-consuming and often-overlooked requirement has a certain appeal to the obsessive bureaucratic mind, any state whose legislature has had the foresight to enact Section 1 on purpose and construction along with the rest of the Act should not be led into such distracting awkwardness. (Continuing Legal Education documents which have noticed this rather alarming possibility include the essay by Robert Surovell in the CLE pamphlet *Child Custody* (Va. State Bar and Bar Assoc., 1980, at V-5), and the very detailed treatment by Melvyn Frumkes in *Support, Custody and Marital Property in Florida* (Fla. State Bar 1981, at 12.) Experience in some states shows, however, that courts frequently ignore the requirement, even in interstate cases. Likewise, the judge is supposed to first check the Interstate Register (See UCCJA Sec. 16) for this case—but whether even one state has set up the register so far remains an interesting question.

The absurdity of the position in which several states now find themselves by virtue of adopting language that makes the Uniform Child Custody Jurisdiction Act, with its Section 9 affidavit requirements, applicable to "all custody cases" is a matter of some justifiable concern. It is arguable that only by requiring the affidavits in all domestic cases can a court be sure whether a case is interstate, but overburdened courts are unlikely to take enthusiastically to any procedure that seems needlessly to multiply the workload. Though one can construe from Section 1 a limitation of all UCCJA provisions to interstate cases, Minnesota, Montana, and New York expressly exclude inappropriate cases by statutory language.

A recent Florida opinion adopts a common-sense solution to part of the somewhat artificial problem in holding that the requirement is at least not jurisdictional. Though the case was a strictly intrastate dependency case, it was argued on appeal that the state's failure to file the UCCJA informational affidavits divested the trial court of jurisdiction. The Florida Court of Appeal for the Fifth District admitted that Florida statutes make the UCCJA applicable to "all custody proceedings," including dependency cases. However, the fact that the affidavits were not filed until six weeks after the initial pleading in the dependency case was filed does not, it was held, void the action taken. Although it is error to proceed without making both sides file the required affidavits, the affidavit requirement of UCCJA Section 9 is not jurisdictional, the court declared, for there is also the provision of UCCJA Section 3 saying that a court of this state has jurisdiction to make child custody determinations if it is the home state. The jurisdictional requirements of the UCCJA, the court said, are those set forth in Section 3. There was other competent evidence to show that Florida qualified for jurisdiction under the UCCJA in this case. (*T.L. v. Florida Department of Health & Rehabilitative Services,* 392 So. 2d 288, 7 FLR 2152 (Fla. Ct. App. 5th Dist. 1980)

The wisdom of effectuating the Act's purposes by granting stays while jurisdiction elsewhere is determined or exercised is discussed in *Bosse, supra; Wise v. Aldrich, supra;* and *Bergstrom v. Bergstrom,* 271 N.W.2d 540, 5 FLR 3001 (N.D. 1978). The availability of an injunction against removing a child from a state is discussed in *Lopez v. District Court,* 606 P.2d 853, 6 FLR 2308 (Colo. 1980). Unsuccessful invocation of Section 11(c)'s travel reimbursement provision can be seen in *Re Mintle,* 294 N.W.2d 564, 6 FLR 2786 (Iowa 1980).

A procedural case which should prove very useful for those seeking to frustrate the workings of the UCCJA's continuing jurisdiction scheme by placing new obstacles in the path of the out-of-state custodial parent who seeks to enforce his foreign decree is *Beck v. Smith,* 296 N.W.2d 886, 6 FLR 2876 (N.D. 1980). The extreme view taken by a majority of the court is that there can be no enforcement of a foreign custody decree until the rather complicated and prolonged procedure of the Uniform Enforcement of Foreign Judgements Act, with its built-in delay of notice-plus-ten-days, is gone through. In so holding, it overrules the prior North Dakota law in *Giddings v. Giddings,* 228 N.W.2d 915, (N.D. 1975).

The Beck case also addresses itself to the matter of temporary stays for purposes of appeal and extraordinary writs, holding, as the court did in *Bergstrom v. Bergstrom, supra,* that generally such stays of a finding of no jurisdiction frustrate the purposes of the Act.

Another creative variation on the theme of UCCJA procedure introduces considerable uncertainty into the interstate scheme. In the very hard case of a convicted murderer's child, *In re Mullins, supra*, the Minnesota Supreme Court realized that it had to let California courts decide whether the boy should return to the allegedly rehabilitated murderer or stay with Minnesota foster parents. However, a majority of the court decided that as the state where the child had resided for five years, Minnesota had a right to condition the boy's return to the west coast on the holding of a Minnesota evidentiary hearing. The only UCCJA provision that authorizes this is the voluntary wording of Section 19, which allows a state in California's position to ask for such a hearing.

## EXCEPTIONS TO CONTINUING JURISDICTION

The basic tool and principle of the entire UCCJA for achieving its aim of providing custodial stability is of course continuing jurisdiction. But obviously continuing jurisdiction in the first decreeing court is far from an ideal answer to the overall problem, and as any statute regulating the care and custody of children must provide for flexibility, the UCCJA necessarily embodies exceptions to that fundamental rule. Some exceptions appear more plainly in the statute itself, such as the acknowledgment of Section 14(a) that a state which had UCCJA Section 3 jurisdiction by virtue of its onetime significant connections might no longer have it. Other exceptions, less obvious from the text, are brought out in the ordeal of adversary litigation.

Some of the best arguments for making an exception to the general anti-forum shopping rule of the UCCJA are those based on defects in the earlier foreign decree, as for example, its procurement by fraud. (See *In re Verbin,* 595 P.2d 905, 5 FLR 2636 (Wash. 1979).) Usually it is a default or other ex parte decree, with the defect being one of notice. In *Fernandez v. Rodriguez,* 411 N.Y.S. 2d 134, 97 Misc. 2d 353 (Monroe Cty. Sup. Ct. 1978), for instance, it was held proper for New York to disregard continuing jurisdiction and take jurisdiction to modify a default custody decree when the Puerto Rican court that rendered it did not have, or at least no longer had, custody under standards like the Uniform Act's. Thus, in the Montana case *In re Pierce,* 601 P.2d 1179, 6 FLR 2028 (1979), recognition was not required when the prior decree was invalid for reasons such as insufficient notice to the losing party, and in *Grubs v. Ross,* 6 FLR 2823, continuing jurisdiction considerations were held to be of little weight in a case where the first state not only had lost its "significant connections" over time, but also had granted its decree ex parte without an adversary hearing (Ore. Ct. App., 8/4/80). Likewise in the *Settle* case (556 P.2d 962, 3 FLR 2181 (Ore. Ct. App. 1976)), it was not just that Indiana had lost its "significant connections" over time, but that Indiana had not had jurisdiction in the first place and its decree never took effect. Similarly, the court in *Wenz v. Schwarze* did not feel obliged to honor the prior decree since it was ex parte.

An opinion of the Illinois Supreme Court in *Siegel v. Siegel*, 7 FLR 3009 (1/20/81), held that neither Section 14(a) of the Act, nor the Illinois version of the UCCJA that lacked that section, supports a theory of continuing jurisdiction that would allow a court to modify its custody decree years after children and custodial parent have moved out of state and all UCCJA Section 3(b) "significant connections" with the original state have dissipated. Even if the modification is only a discharge of the father's child support obligations as a sanction for the mother's denial of visitation, this is still true, the Illinois Supreme Court held. The reason is that UCCJA continuing jurisdiction exists in a decreeing state only when basic Section 3 jurisdiction still exists, it explained. This was a reversal of the holding at 400 N.E.2d 6, 6 FLR 2168.

The great underlying question troubling probably all those who contemplate the UCCJA theory and scheme is whether the continuing jurisdiction principle is so important that it should dictate honoring the jurisdiction that a foreign state acquired by virtue of a unilateral removal and a court decision that seems to ill accord with UCCJA principles. The question was squarely faced by the California Court of Appeal for the First District in *Hopson v. Hopson*, 6 FLR 2952 (10/6/80). The court held that a trial court should not have given "full faith and credit" to a Tennessee decree which modified an Arizona decree by changing custody of the child from the mother to the father. Tennessee, the California Appellate Court held, was not the home state at the time. The children had lived in California before the father took them from there to Tennessee, and the California Appellate Court attaches no significance to the fact that the children had been in California only because the mother had moved them there in defiance of a express prohibition in the Arizona decree. The Tennessee decree, the court said, runs afoul of the "clean hands" principle by legitimizing the child-snatcher's custody so that he would profit by his own wrong. The court went on to explain that it did not have to honor the Tennessee decree under the registration provisions of the UCCJA, since it was marred by the underlying lack of jurisdiction and since (although the California court was in error here, since Tennessee had had the UCCJA for quite some time) that Tennessee jurisdiction had been taken under jurisdictional standards very different from those of the UCCJA. More importantly, the court said that a child brought to a state in violation of a foreign custody order should not acquire UCCJA "significant connections" with the new state by continuing to reside there.

In *Baird v. Baird*, 374 So.2d 60, 5 FLR 2812, it was held that the earlier foreign decree was properly disregarded in an Arizona father's petition for enforcement, since the Arizona decision against the relocating custodial mother—transferring custody to the father—had been made only after she had left the state and when her legal representation in Arizona may have been inadequate.

Initially it would seem difficult to cast UCCJA issues as part of the ideological struggle between feminism and whatever its opposite is—except that for some the fact that most custodial parents are female is enough to make possible the taking of a feminist stance on these issues. Those partisans of single-parent autonomy who are able to see the UCCJA as primarily an assertion of custodial over non-custodial parents' rights and see enforcement of visitation rights as a reactionary political act have argued for the creation of a new, unwritten exception to the UCCJA. It is to the effect that a "punitive decree"—defined as one which "punitively" remedies, by changing custody, a custodial parent's defiance of a custody decree's visitation provisions—need not be honored. This argument was tried and failed in *Re Lemond*, 395 N.E.2d 1287, 6 FLR 2045 (Ind. Ct. App. 1st Dist. 1979) despite its articulation as a component of a parent's constitutional right to travel (and transport children). Though it has been held to be a principle under the UCCJA that custody should not be modified solely as a device for punishing a defiant custodial parent who destroys visitation rights (see Commissioners' Notes, 9 Uniform Laws Annotated 155 (1979), and *Ehr v. Ehr*, 396 N.E.2d 87, 6 FLR 2127 (Ill. App. Ct. 2d Dist., 1979)), decisions of the criticized class are often simply the result of a court's sober and advised decision that it would be in the best interest of the child to be placed with the parent who will try to preserve for his child some access to both parents, and the practical acknowledgment that custody rights are easier to enforce interstate than visitation rights. (Incidentally, Section 2(2) does contemplate the use of the UCCJA to enforce visitation rights.) Custody decrees are still properly based on all relevant factors touching upon a child's welfare, and as the Indiana Court of Appeals in *Lemond* explains, even if it is assumed that a decree issued for no other reason than to punish a parent has some kind of second-class citizenship entitling it to "less than total deference," still, a court under the UCCJA has no business assuming that a modification decree was issued for such reasons, rather than to benefit the child.

There has, however, been court recognition of the existence of something called a "punitive decree" which merits less than full deference under the Uniform Act. However, that acknowledgment was of something far different from what anti-visitation partisans contemplate. The court in *Brooks v. Brooks,* 530 P.2d 547 (Ore. Ct. App., 1975), like the courts in the cases cited above, said that a "punitive decree" was one which was issued to punish the conduct of one parent or reward the other without any evidence on the relevant issues having been taken. Thus in *Brooks* the creation of a "punitive decree" theory to justify an exception to the UCCJA Section 14 rule against modification of prior custody decrees by courts still having jurisdiction was simply the creation of a different label for the phenomenon perceived in such cases as *Pierce, Grubs,* and *Wenz, supra.* The court in *Settle v. Settle,* 550 P.2d 445 (Ore. Ct. App. 1976, reversed on other grounds 556 P.2d 962) defined a punitive decree as one granted *only* because the court is insulted at one parent's disregard of its authority. The court in *Miller v. Superior Court,* 587 P.2d 723, 5 FLR 2228 (Cal. 1978), declined the invitation to create a "punitive decree" exception.

## SIMILAR STATE LAW EXCEPTION

The Uniform Child Custody Jurisdiction Act is not a reciprocal statute, requiring enactment by the foreign state as a prerequisite for according comity to its judgments, but perhaps it comes close to being that sort of statute in its requirement that the other state being deferred to have "similar" jurisdictional law. For instance, Section 3(a)(4) allows forum-state jurisdiction if "it appears that no other state would have jurisdiction under prerequisites substantially in accordance with" those of the UCCJA. A similar formulation is found in Section 6 on avoidance of simultaneous proceedings, Section 13 providing for recognition of foreign decrees, and Section 14 forbidding their modification. This has been of relatively little consequence because virtually all the states have been exercising similar comity law with and without the UCCJA, and in most respects the remaining non-UCCJA states could be said to have similar jurisdictional law despite non-enactment. The drafting Uniform State Laws Commissioners say in their commentary (Page 20) that in using this formulation they purposely left open the possibility of according comity to states which themselves treat comity as a discretionary alternative rather than a mandatory obligation. The fact that the statute is not reciprocal as such was mentioned in *Re Bacon, supra,* which added that UCCJA's allowing a state to honor decrees from states which do not have the UCCJA does not make the Act unconstitutional.

However, the requirement of similar state jurisdictional law has sometimes been significant. In *Fernandez v. Rodriguez, supra,* for instance, the Puerto Rico decree did not have to be honored because the island's jurisdictional standards were not substantially like those of the Uniform Act, and it was held that Puerto Rico had exercised jurisdiction in a way that did not meet the fairness requirements of the Act—sufficient prior notice being one conspicuously absent factor. In *Clark v. Clark,* 404 N.E.2d 23 (Ind. Ct. App. 1st Dist., 1980), the court stressed, in calling a pre-UCCJA Kentucky determination qualified for recognition under the Act, that the Commissioners' introduction to the Act calls it non-reciprocal.

And yet, the variations in the version of the UCCJA that Kentucky adopted were held to have fatal effect in *Howard v. Howard,* 378 So.2d 1329, 6 FLR 2241 (Fla. Ct. App. 5th Dist., 1980). The court said that Florida need not honor a Kentucky decree when Kentucky, under its then selective version of the Act, did not have jurisdiction under Kentucky law (because the child was not physically present there) when it rendered its decree. Similarly, in *Pasqualone v. Pasqualone,* 406 N.E.2d 1121, 6 FLR 2744 (1980), the Ohio Supreme Court held that Illinois should not be treated as a state having similar jurisdictional law, despite its apparent adoption of the UCCJA, since the Illinois adoption was so partial and selective, leaving out key elements of the UCCJA scheme. It was probably through careful attention on counsel's part to the exact wording of the foreign statute that these discrepancies were discovered and the court persuaded in each case to accord them so much weight. The exception was invoked by a California court against Tennessee in *Hopson v. Hopson, supra.*

## EMERGENCY, RELATED EXCEPTIONS

The exception to general UCCJA comity principles which is written into Section 3(a)(3) is one that many lawyers seeking forum-state jurisdiction may turn to as a first resort, and already it has been a fruitful source of UCCJA litigation producing appellate opinions. It allows finding jurisdiction over a child physically present in the state who has been abandoned or needs to be protected from the threat of mistreatment, abuse, neglect or (bracketed) "dependency" in an emergency situation. This jurisdiction ground applies notwithstanding other jurisdictional limitations of the Act, but remains subject to qualification by the Section 7 forum non conveniens provision. The Commissioners in their notes stressed that this jurisdiction "is reserved for extraordinary circumstances," giving as an example *In re Lang,* 193 N.Y.S.2d 763 (1959), and cautioned that non-emergency "child neglect" will not qualify. (For more recent declarations of this see *Trujillo v. Trujillo,* 378 So.2d 812 (Fla. Ct. App. 3d Dist., 1979), and *Constantino v. Constantino, supra.*

Though emergency is, relatively speaking, a frequently raised objection, it is apparently seldom successful. An "emergency" as contemplated by the exception was found by the Georgia Supreme Court in *Webb v. Webb, supra,* cert. granted 6 FLR 2945, in a parent's leaving a child alone and unattended in an arguably dangerous environment. It was likewise found in an Illinois mother's physical abuse of the child in *Breneman v. Breneman,* 284 N.W.2d 804, 6 FLR 2074 (Mich. Ct. App., 1979). It was held to outweigh forum non conveniens considerations in *Ferreira v. Ferreira,* 512 P.2d 304 (Calif. 1973), and in *Moser v. Davis,* 364 So.2d 521, 5 FLR 2207 (Fla. Ct. App. 2d Dist., 1978). The fact that children present in the state alleged physical violence was considered to be enough to justify Florida in taking jurisdiction for purposes of inquiring. Just how such a claim ought to be handled is usefully discussed in *Kern v. Kern,* 150 Cal. Rptr. 860, 87 Cal. App. 3d 402, 5 FLR 2169 (Cal. Ct. App. 1st Dist., 1978): if there seems a possibility that a child's physical safety could be in grave danger upon release to a non-resident custodial parent, it was said, the court should do no more than to grant temporary custody to the resident parent while the matter is inquired into. For a case stating how cautious a court must be even if it does find emergency, see *In re Thomas,* 573 P.2d 1095 (Colo. 1975). *Marcrum v. Marion County Superior Court,* 403 N.E.2d 806 (Ind. 1980), emphasizes that this provision is not triggered by a parent's mere self-serving declarations.

Unsuccessful claims of emergency, abandonment and danger to children do seem to be the more common. In *Woodhouse v. District Court,* 587 P.2d 1199, 5 FLR 2253 (Colorado 1978), the father's self-serving statements that the child "appeared unwell" were not enough to invoke the exception. And in *Brock v. District Court,* 620 P.2d 11, 7 FLR 2035 (1980), the Colorado Supreme Court, adding that it takes a "grave" and "compelling" emergency to defeat continuing jurisdiction, held that a father's psychological and psychiatric reports showing that the child was "hyperactive" and "experiencing a childhood adjustment disorder" did not rise to that level (citing in support *Roberts v. District Court,* 596 P.2d 65, 5 FLR 2901 (1979); *Wilson v. Wilson,* 474 P.2d 789 (1970); and *In re Thomas, supra.*) The New York court in *R. v. H.*, 410 Misc. 2d 53 (1978), may have inaugurated a useful concept when it said, in rejecting an emergency claim, that a child's being allegedly unhappy in Michigan and allegedly not properly cared for there did not present a crisis situation. So important were UCCJA comity principles to the Pennsylvania Superior Court for the Pittsburgh district in *Zaubi v. Zaubi,* 6 FLR 2306, (affirmed 423 A.2d 333, 7 FLR 2055) that alleged dangers of sexual abuse by the child's grandfather at her new European residence were held to be outweighed by the policy against child-snatching, even though the allegations were based on uncontested evidence and even though the child-snatching took place only after the Danish mother in whose favor the court decided had snatched her first.

In perhaps a typical emergency-claim case, the Illinois Appellate Court for the Second District declined to exercise the concurrent jurisdiction that it had, and refused to find the contemplated danger to the child in the mother's promiscuous and vagabond life, her marijuana use, and her frustration of the father's visitation rights. *Ehr v. Ehr,* 396 N.E.2d 87, 6 FLR 2127 (1979).

*In re Schwander,* 145 Cal. Rptr. 325, 4 FLR 2467 (Calif. Ct. App. 2d Dist., 4/18/78), represents a rejection of both "emergency" and "punitive decree" exceptions. There the forum state deferred to continuing jurisdiction because the proof of alleged "emergency"—though invited—was never forthcoming at all. The danger-to-child exception was recognized but disregarded in the rather confused Montana case *In re Pierce,* 601 P.2d 1179, 6 FLR 2028 (1979). Intriguingly, the court there decided that the interaction of the Interstate Compact on Juveniles and the UCCJA left the Montana trial court barred from modifying the previous Wyoming custody order, but able to ignore it. Since the Interstate Compact allowed the Montana court to deny, on grounds of child-abuse prevention, the Wyoming order that the child be returned there, the child was allowed to stay with Montana grandparents and thus effectively taken from her out-of-state parents. In *De Passe v. De Passe,* 421 N.Y.S. 2d 497, 6 FLR 2108 (N.Y. App. Div. 4th Dept., 1979), a case similar to *Ehr*, the rejected emergency claim was of the father's heavy drinking and excessive spending. The usual pattern of courts being asked to apply the emergency provisions, but holding that to apply them in the circumstances would nullify the purposes of the Act, shows up in such cases as *Young v. District Court,* 570 P.2d 249, 4 FLR 2013 (Colo. 1977; *Roberts v. District Court,* 596 P.2d 65, 5 FLR 2901 (Colo. 1979); and *In re Irene R.,* 5 FLR 2635 (N.Y. Fam. Ct. Westchester Cty., 5/14/79). In *Winkleman v. Moses,* 249 N.W.2d 897, 5 FLR 2709 (S.D. 1979), the emergency contention was rejected over a vigorous dissent. *Kern v. Kern, supra,* is useful in explaining that even when the emergency is found, it should result only in a temporary custody award.

## BEST INTEREST EXCEPTION?

One of the unsettling things about the *Baird* case, *supra*, is that, very near the end of the opinion, after holding that Florida was indeed the child's home state; that the mother's bringing the child there could not be considered wrongful; and that the Arizona proceedings, begun after she left and conducted ex parte, did not require exercise of Florida's concurrent jurisdiction to be declined, the appellate court seemed to determine the entire question by stating with approval that the court below "simply declined to enforce the Arizona decree on the basis that [sic] the best interest of the child requires her continued presence with the mother." What decisions such as this may unfortunately indicate is that despite the careful wording of the Act a significant number of trial court judges still think that after all of its verbiage has been given lip service, the decision on jurisdiction ultimately resolves itself into one of "best interest"—i.e., not a jurisdictional decision to all. At least the idea may well be abroad that ultimately a simple, unadorned "best interest of the child" concept is in itself an exception to all UCCJA anti-forum-shopping principles. Although the wording of Section 3 carefully avoids any justifiable impression that that is the rule, it does make best interest of the child one factor in the complex calculus. Apparently that is sometimes seized on, creating an unjustified impression. A hint of a new exception was conveyed by the Georgia Supreme Court in *Webb, supra,* when it said that the local court was right to accept jurisdiction despite a pending Florida action because the forum non conveniens considerations included "judicial economy" in having the case decided immediately rather than bounced back to another state. There were in that case, however, other factors such as arguable emergency endangering the child. (See the dissent, 6 FLR 2537.)

Best interest of the child, when combined with "most information" home state, significant connection, and forum non conveniens factors, was held to prevail over "clean hands" considerations in *Bosse v. Superior Court,* 152 Cal. Rptr. 665, 89 Cal. App. 3d 440 (Calif. Ct. App. 1st Dist. 1979). In *Neal v. Superior Court,* 148 Cal. Rptr. 841, 5 FLR 2072 (Calif. Ct. App. 2d Dist. 1978), it was noted in passing that the mere claim that "California is better for the child's health", added to a "most information" claim, was not sufficient to prevail over clean hands considerations.

Of course these cases serve to remind courts that slavish homage to the importance of judges' decrees is not more important than the long-run welfare of the children whose interests motivated the Act's passage. It was held in *Giddings, supra,* that it is error to determine jurisdiction without having permitted testimony on best interest.

## BEST INTEREST AND NEW HOME

It has been characterized as making an exception to the UCCJA to treat long residence in the second state, even after a child-snatching, as a compelling circumstance justifying an exception to continuing jurisdiction and clean hands considerations. But the matter becomes little more than semantic, for this is usually nothing but the determination under Sections 13 and 14 and Section 3 that a former home state or prior decree-issuing state has lost, through the disappearance of Section 3 "significant connections" over time, the jurisdiction that it once had. Examples can be seen in *Settle v. Settle, supra* and *Clark, supra.* The same thinking may take the form of a decision that acquisition of a new home state in the forum makes the forum a more convenient one when to hold otherwise would apply the UCCJA's continuing jurisdiction principles in an unjustly forced and draconian manner and stand the UCCJA upon its head. See *Howard v. Gish,* 373 A.2d 1280, 3 FLR 2575 (Md. Ct. Spec. App. 1977)). But it was also emphasized in *Paltrow v. Paltrow,* 376 A.2d 1134, 3 FLR 2716 (Md. Ct. Spec. App., 1977), that even a real "second home state" should not assume jurisdiction absent "compelling circumstances" if this would conflict with a prior decree from another state.

But perhaps the most significant court statement on the place that "best interest" plays in the entire scheme is found in *Clark v. Clark,* 404 N.E.2d 23 (Ind. Ct. App. 1st Dist., 1980), which declares that the two principal purposes of the Uniform Act are discouraging forum shopping and protecting children's best interests (citing *Settle, supra,* and *Brock v. Brock,* 349 So. 2d 782 (Fla. Ct. App. 1977)), and that "when a factual situation presents an irreconcilable conflict between promoting the orderly system of decisions and protecting the best interests of the child before the court, the Act makes predominant the best interests of the child."

## OTHER EXCEPTIONS—DEFICIENT DECREE

An example of a case in which the new state will in fact accept jurisdiction, because there never was a custody decree in the original divorcing state (but rather, only a divorce decree which did not mention custody of the children) is *In re Rose M.S.,* 6 FLR 2920, (N.Y. Fam. Ct. Kings Cty., 10/1/80). Perhaps a classic example of the "deficient foreign decree" case is *In re Donovan R,* 5 FLR 2845 (Calif. Ct. App. 1st Dist., 7/26/79), in which the foreign decree was held not to have been issued under jurisdictional standards like those of the UCCJA—notice having been conspicuously lacking. It was also held that continuing jurisdiction dissipated because the significant connections had been lost by the original state and acquired by the new home state.

In *Re Gomez,* 6 FLR 2903, (N.Y. Sup. Ct. Queens Cty., 9/19/80), a trial court decided to give recognition to the significant connections possessed by the new home state when the original decree had issued from a court (a) in a state lacking significant connections, (b) affording no adversary hearing and (c) not exploring the child's best interest.

The New York court thus decided to assume jurisdiction and exercise it even though it was child-snatching that brought the child into the forum state, since the Section 8 equities seemed to balance out and the original-forum decree itself resulted from an act amounting to uncleanliness of hands. On the other hand, a sensitive distinction was made by the Colorado Supreme Court when it declared in *Kraft v. District Court,* 593 P.2d 321, 5 FLR 2318 (1979), that it would not make an exception for the foreign decree's having been ex-parte when the reason for that was the mother's having fled with the child to the foreign state. Colorado therefore deferred to Nebraska, even though Nebraska did not at that time have the UCCJA.

## POSITIVE USE

The UCCJA generally works well to effect its major purpose of preventing the greatest interjurisdictional outrage: the legitimation in a new state of the child snatching that the losing party in a custody contest has resorted to. However, the most distressing cases nowadays are those in which the child-snatcher makes no attempt to legitimize his custody, but simply hides out in the other state with no plans of going into court. The Act, however, is designed to reach these cases as well, and can be used affirmatively, as a sword rather than a shield. Thus aggrieved custodial parents do not have to wait passively until the party who has violated the custody decree goes into court.

Sections 13 and 15–19 of the Act provide for enforcing the custody decrees of other states, and their careful draftmanship pays considerable attention to the mechanics of the enforcement system. The operation of the Act in this way is sufficiently clear and automatic that there is very little room for lawyer argument or difference of opinion among judges, and obviously very little appellate law is made.

One opinion imposing a major roadblock in the path of custodial parents seeking to use the registration and enforcement provisions, however, is the creative opinion of the majority in *Beck v. Smith,* discussed *supra,* setting up a severely troublesome impediment to affirmative use of the UCCJA as a sword for victimized custodial parents. The North Dakota Supreme Court said that it found support for grafting the UEFJA onto the UCCJA enforcement provision in something the Commissioners said rather offhandedly in their commentary.

Discussing application of Section 13 on recognition and enforcement of foreign decrees, the Oregon Court of Appeals in *Butler v. Morgan,* 578 P.2d 814, 4 FLR 2538 (1978), declared it was proper to use habeas corpus, and to seek enforcement of the out-of-state decree by contempt. The Act, the court said, did not destroy pre-existing enforcement measures such as habeas corpus. It was agreed by the court in *Mitchell v. Pincock,* 577 P.2d 343, 4 FLR 2336 (Idaho 1978), that habeas corpus was appropriate for this purpose.

## INTERNATIONAL APPLICATION

That the drafters of the Act intended it to apply to international cases is clear: Section 23, "International Application" says that "the general policies of this Act extend to the international area" (perhaps short for *arena*) and a second sentence adds that the Act's provisions for recognition and enforcement of out-of-state decrees apply to foreign-country decrees issued by either judicial or administrative authorities who accord both sides reasonable notice and hearing opportunity. The wording of the second sentence is untypically obscure, but is clarified by the drafters' commentary. That commentary also appears to dispense with any notion that the foreign-country procedural or substantive custody law need be at all similar to American law in any way beyond notice and hearing requirements. It goes on to explain specifically that the foreign tribunal need have had jurisdiction only under its own law, rather than UCCJA Section 3 jurisdiction.

This appears to impose very few limits on giving effect to decrees of foreign states that have radically different custody laws and very different ideas of legitimate jurisdiction over a custody case. Now most cases reported seem to concern other countries with an English common-law heritage, in virtually all of which the substantive custody standard is indeed the best interest of the child. However, the number of cases coming from countries with very different jurisdictional and substantive ideas is likely to grow. This raises the problem of conflict between the position taken in the Section 23 commentary and the requirement of Section 14, providing that those decrees deserving to be given continuing-jurisdiction effect are those from states which take jurisdiction "under jurisdictional prerequisites substantially in accordance with this Act."

The Commissioners explained in their Section 23 commentary that they were deferring to the jurisdictional notions of other countries because that is the general principle of international conflicts of laws. Section 14's commentary seems to include no explanation of the "similarity" requirement. Though this section is not often construed, the Act has been internationally applied in a number of cases, including *Zaubi v. Zaubi,* 5 FLR 2306 (Pa. Super. Ct. Pitts. Dist, 2/27/80, affirmed 7 FLR 2055); *Miller v. Superior Court,* 587 P.2d 723, 5 FLR 2228 (Calif. 1978); *Woodhouse v. District Court,* 587 P.2d

1199, 5 FLR 2253 (Colo. 1978); *In re Shalit*, 4 FLR 2035 (N.Y. Sup. Ct. N.Y. Cty. 1977); *Taylor v. Taylor*, (Pa. Super. Ct. Phila. Dist., 5/30/80); and in *Bergstrom v. Bergstrom*, and *In re Ben Yehoshua*, both *supra*.

The decision in *Shalit* required return of a child to England and the court in *Zaubi* recognized and enforced a Danish decree. The court in *Woodhouse* considered the problem of similar law and, after carefully considering whether England's 1973 Matrimonial Causes Act constitutes similar law for UCCJA purposes, held that it does. In *Miller v. Superior Court*, there was sharp dispute about the point, for the losing party and three dissenting judges of the California Supreme Court argued that Australia's issuance of a decree without notice or hearing made the law less than similar, or at least should have come within the "no notice" exception to the Act's continuing jurisdiction rule.

In *Re Anne A. (Re Agbasi)*, 6 FLR 2876, (N.Y. Fam. Ct. Bronx Cty., 9/10/80), significant connections were found and New York jurisdiction found and exercised even though the boy in question had been taken to Nigeria by the father. One factor was that the father had seen fit to leave the boy's several siblings in New York.

## VARIATIONS

As UCCJA enactment becomes nationwide and litigation more common, the issue of individual state tailoring of the Uniform Act becomes more crucial. Many states, for instance, have rewritten the Commissioners' carefully-drafted notice provisions, often to conform to the general existing state law. Perhaps unwittingly, some of them have created severe difficulties for those trying to use the Act for its intended purposes in some special situations—such as international cases—by deleting the provisions for service by mail.

Several states, including Florida, Ohio, South Dakota, and Virginia have decided to do without the Section 1 statement of purposes and interpretation principles. However, it is difficult, with resort to the purpose clause being so frequent, to see how a court could with intellectual rigor adhere to that kind of legislative declaration. The South Dakota Supreme Court, for one, has announced that the deletion makes no difference, and has read the entire text of Section 1 into *Winkleman v. Moses*, 279 N.W.2d 897, 5 FLR 2709 (1979), to stand as judge-made law.

The statement in Section 1 of the Act's general principles and purposes, and of the requirement that all other sections be construed in accordance with them, has proved quite useful to construing courts, particularly where there appears to be a conflict between the benevolent aims of the UCCJA as stated in its various sections. It was instructively resorted to in *Roberts v. District Court,* 596 P.2d 65 (Colo. 1979); *In re Settle,* 550 P.2d 445, (Ore. Ct. App. 1976; reversed on other grounds, 556 P.2d 962, 3 FLR 2181 (1976)); *In re Rector,* 565 P.2d 950 (Colo. 1977); *Brock v. Brock, supra; Fry v. Ball,* 544 P.2d 402, 2 FLR 2169 (Colo 1975); *Neal v. Superior Court,* 84 Cal. 3d 847, 148 Cal. Rptr. 841, 5 FLR 2072 (Calif. Ct. App. 2d Dist. 1978); *Clark v. Clark,* 404 N.E.2d 23 (Ind. Ct. App. 1st Dist., 1980); and *Lovko v. Lovko,* 384 N.E.2d 166 (Ind. Ct. App. 2d Dist. 1978).

One of the most disconcerting effects of state-by-state tailoring, however, is that variations in the Act can keep one state's version from being "similar law" for purposes of recognition under Section 3(a)(4), Section 6(a), Section 13, and Section 14. This creates just one more opportunity for an unsympathetic local court to refuse to honor another state's decree and nullify the reform initiative that the Act represents. This happened in *Pasqualone v. Pasqualone,* 406 N.E.2d 1121, 6 FLR 2744 (Ohio 1980), and the effect of (now-abandoned) Kentucky variations (See *Freeman v. Freeman,* 547 S.W.2d 437, 3 FLR 2233) was fatal in *Howard v. Howard,* 378 So.2d 1329, 6 FLR 2241 (Fla. Ct. App. 5th Dist., 1980). Of course judicial construction can create significant variations too, as for example in the Georgia Supreme Court's apparent declaration in *Yearta v. Scroggins,* 268 S.E.2d 151, 6 FLR 2644 (1980), that the Act does not cover any case arising out of a request for custody modification. Some states have expressed an intention consistent with UCCJA adoption, but have been very selective indeed. Kentucky in 1977 adopted only the jurisdiction section of the Act, incorporating it into its version of the Uniform Marriage & Divorce Act. (See Ky. Rev. Stat. Ann. §403.260 (Baldwin Supp. 1977).) Later, in 1980, SB42 was enacted and approved, adopting the whole Act.

Texas was even more particular in its local domestication of the Act when it adopted the scheme now embodied in §§ 11.045, 11.051, 11.052, and 11.053 of its Family Code. There has been both minor and major Texanization, but § 11.045 was inspired by and comes close to UCCJA Section 3 on jurisdiction. Sections 12 and 13 on res judicata and non-modification are approximated by §§11.051 and 11.052, but there are some significant differences. Section 11.051, a long-arm statute, embodies some aspects of UCCJA Section 3 jurisdiction.

Alaska's election to do without Section 3(a)(2) "significant connection" jurisdiction could cause a similar "non-similarity" finding, but apparently has not yet. For a discussion of Illinois variations see *Pasqualone, supra,* and *Siegel, infra.*

## NEW ISSUES, NEW USES

The new case-law interpretations of the Uniform Child Custody Jurisdiction Act are also testing the limits of the statute's applicability in putting little-noticed provisions of the Act to use. It should be noted that the UCCJA in Section 2(2) specifically applies itself to visitation controversies, and thus it has been used for visitation enforcement (see *Siegel v. Siegel,* 400 N.E.2d 6, 6 FLR 2168 (Ill. App. Ct. 1st Dist, 1979), reversed 7 FLR 3009) and against the custodial parent in relocation cases. In *Policastro v. Policastro,* 5 FLR 2427, it was invoked to protect the visitation rights of the father when the mother sought to move away in violation of separation agreement provisions (N.Y. Sup. Ct. Suffolk Cty, 2/6/79). (Some other custodial-parent relocation cases in which the forum issue was decided under the UCCJA include *Lopez v. District Court,* 606 P.2d 853, 6 FLR 2308 (Colo. 1980) and *In re Woods,* 6 FLR 2175 (Calif. Ct. App. 1st Dist. (unpublished) 1/27/79). *In re Nichols* (N.Y. A.D. 6/26/80) emphasized that the applicability to visitation is found right in the text of the Act and as *Ehr v. Ehr,* 396 N.E.2d 87, 6 FLR 2127 (Ill. App. Ct. 2d Dist. 1979), pointed out, the Commissioners' notes themselves state (9 ULA 155 (1979)) that it is a principle of the UCCJA that custody should not be modified as a way of punishing frustration of visitation rights. (A simplistic extrapolation from this sound principle and an expansionist reading of the "no adversary hearing" cases give rise to the "punitive decree exception" philosophy, discussed elsewhere.)

*Bahr v. Galonski,* 257 N.W.2d 869 (Wis. 1977), declared that the anti-tampering and res judicata provisions of Sections 12 and 14 of the Act do not mean that the courts cannot adjust visitation rights that are embodied in a foreign decree. In *Smith v. Superior Court,* 137 Cal. Rptr. 348, 68 Cal App. 3d 457 (Calif. Ct. App. 1st Dist. 1977), the opinion voiced a similar recognition. The Act was used by a New York court to get visitation with a child presently living in New Jersey when both the plaintiff grandmother and the defendant father were New York residents in *Louise G. v. Peter C.,* 411 N.Y.S. 2d 101, 97 Misc. 2d 338 (N.Y. Fam. Ct. Kings Cty. 1978).

Attempts to use the Uniform Child Custody Jurisdiction Act intrastate have failed, as in *Adams v. Adams,* 374 So.2d 29, 5 FLR 2776 (Fla. Ct. App. 3d Dist. 1979), and in *Zamaludin v. Ishoof,* 409 A.2d 1118, 6 FLR 2218 (Md. Ct. Spec. App. 1980). Of course it is not foreclosed to a state to enact an intrastate child custody jurisdiction act to solve some of its intercounty problems, such as Pennsylvania (see *J.C.S. v. D.M.S.,* 6 FLR 2526 (Pa. Super. Ct., 5/16/80)), and Georgia (see *Yearta v. Scroggins, supra;* and *Brock v. District Court,* 620 P.2d 11, 7 FLR 3035 (Colo. 10/27/80)) have done.

The Act was used in *Re Jacqueline F.* 391 N.E.2d 967, 5 FLR 2636 (N.Y. 1979), to force counsel for a child-snatching parent to reveal the child's location.

The Act has also been used against natural parents in a parental rights termination context in *Wenz v. Schwarze*, 598 P.2d 1089, 5 FLR 2813 (Mont. 1979), and in *Re Quenzer*, 599 P.2d 121, 5 FLR 2969 (Ore. Ct. App. 1979), for alimony enforcement.

It is probable that many of the new issues to arise under the UCCJA will grow out of the existing problem of partial and selective adoption by the various states. It may be that in at least some of the states, despite the historical tendency of statutory reaction in the opposite direction, legislative reform will be directed toward eliminating these local tailorings and re-standardizing the UCCJA nationwide.

Certainly the Uniform Child Custody Jurisdiction Act cannot be all things to all persons and cannot overcome the problems raised by prejudice, corruption, human error, and scarcity of resources, and the parent who seeks to invoke the Act in a distant state after being victimized by child snatching faces an uphill battle. Invoking the legal processes in another state can be very awkward without a lawyer and very expensive with one. The indigent parent is at a distinct disadvantage and the parent who is not indigent at first may soon become so. Since legal aid agencies are hardly ever of any use to the litigant from outside even the city or county which funds them, many parents will still be frustrated until some kind of requirement for providing legal aid to non-residents is written into the Act. It should be noted that the Uniform Reciprocal Enforcement of Support Act, and the International Convention on the Abduction of Children by Parents, do attempt to bridge this gap.

Given the sheer weight of the rhetorical offensive behind it, a significant amount of new litigation may be directed toward the creation of a "right-to-travel" or "punitive decree" exception to the Act's continuing jurisdiction principles in order to keep those principles of the Act from being used to preserve visitation opportunities. Unfortunately, since the custody decisions being complained of are against custodial parents wanting to relocate their children and custodial parents are usually women, there is no denying that this has been perceived politically as a women's rights issue and the proliferation of litigation has this impetus behind it. However, short of writing specific language into the Act legislatively, it is difficult to see how this effort, relying on the theory of an unwritten exception, perhaps supported to a degree by an aside in the Commissioners' commentary to Sections 8 and 13 to the effect that custody modifications should not be used solely to punish a visitation-denying parent, can get very far in the courts. In fact, there will always remain those cases in which a custodial parent—and it must be remembered that an increasing number of them now are male—persistently defies orders of the original decree-issuing court that he afford visitation to a perfectly fit non-custodial parent who only narrowly missed winning the original custody battle, and the court in its decretion ultimately decides that a custody change is the only way the children will ever be afforded the chance of access to both parents. After all, a custody decree is easier to enforce across state lines or national boundaries than a visitation right is, and the non-custodial parent to whom the custody is switched will probably have promised, and can be made to give security for that promise, that he or she will do a better job of respecting visitation rights than the defiant custodial parent has done. In the midst of an earnest campaign to secure uniform interpretation of such a well-meaning, comprehensive, and rationalized statute as the UCCJA, the creation of common-law exceptions could be seen as an unfortunate retrograde development. See the rejection of an argument for the new exception in *Re Lemond*, 395 N.E.2d 1287, 6 FLR 2045 (Ind. Ct. App. 1st Dist 1979).

Another reform that may someday be achieved through the Commissioners or by direct resort to individual state legislatures would address the problem of the military and diplomatic family living abroad. The Uniform Child Custody Jurisdiction Act was designed primarily to assure that too many states do not try to exercise jurisdiction in one child's custody case, but since the UCCJA displaces the previous law and preempts the entire field of regulating interstate custody litigation when a state adopts it, it also has to address the problem of seeing that at least one state somewhere takes the responsibility for deciding the custody of an American child. Though Section 23 would appear to make the foreign country the appropriate state to exercise jurisdiction over persons living there, a host country's courts may be both inappropriate and unwilling to decide disputes about the custody and visitation of children who are living there in an American community or compound as the dependents of American citizens stationed there on military or diplomatic orders. While they might assume jurisdiction when both parents are living in the foreign country with the children and one seeks to invoke their divorce jurisdiction, they are less likely to entertain the case when the parent who is seeking some court to accept the case is the one who is back in the United States. A parent who seeks to defy an American state court's custody or visitation orders can see to it that while the significant connections with the last home state or continuing-jurisdiction state wither away, no significant connections with any new American state are acquired. This proves to be a highly useful device for those seeking to elude the authority of

American courts while enjoying all the other benefits of American citizenship. It can lead to excruciatingly painful results for American parents and children.

The military father who takes children away to his next overseas assignment in defiance of an existing custody order or even a mere separation agreement provision on custody is one example. The armed services themselves are unlikely to do anything to facilitate exercise of American court jurisdiction over this parent. At least the question whether command cooperation will be forthcoming is likely to be a function of the parent's military rank. There seems to be no good reason why the military or diplomatic families should slip through the net. Federal legislation already assures that these Americans neither gain nor lose residency by virtue of being stationed abroad (see Soldiers' and Sailors' Civil Relief Act of 1940, 50 U.S.C. App. 501 et seq.), and the federal and state governments cooperate to assure that the adults stationed abroad do not escape the obligation to pay state income taxes, so it seems simple enough to assign such families to some American state for UCCJA purposes. It is very unrealistic to say that the concurrent-jurisdiction and court-communication provisions of the UCCJA operate to remove these problems, considering the difficulty and expense of trying to communicate with a foreign court in a foreign language.

Interestingly, one non-UCCJA state's statutory attempt to do something about the problem was held improper and unenforceable by a trial court in the New York case. In *Fernandez v. Rodriguez*, 411 N.Y.S.2d 134, 97 Misc. 2d 353 (Monroe Cty. Sup. Ct. 1978), the court said that it did not have to honor a Puerto Rican decree because Puerto Rico did not have jurisdictional statutes substantially similar to the UCCJA. The problem was that Puerto Rico had a statute, 31 LPRA Section 9, declaring that "laws relating to family rights and obligations, or the status, condition and legal capacity of persons, shall be binding on citizens of Puerto Rico, although they reside in a foreign country." Insufficient notice by the Puerto Rican Court was an additional reason for refusal of comity.

Even obtaining service on the military person can be a nightmare. The UCCJA apparently seeks to avoid this by providing for service by mail (Section 5), but at least one state has deleted the service-by-mail provision of Section 5. Maryland omits Section 5 entirely, and at least two states have entirely reworded Section 5 to conform it to their existing state statutes on service of process. Without postal service, Section 5 contemplates personal delivery of papers abroad by a process server, but the pre-UCCJA law is that personal service outside the state is equal only to publication service and the constitutional law is apparently that personal service is necessary in custody cases. When the UCCJA entirely redefines service for its own purposes in Section 5, at least the first of these objections is answered, but tampering negates this effect. Also, at least one European country, West Germany, has recently lodged diplomatic protests with the U.S. under the Hague Convention on service of process, taking the position that off-base personal service of American pleadings on American servicemen on German soil violates its national sovereignty.

Such national reactions could almost entirely destroy international ("quasi international", in the case of denizens of American compounds) application of the UCCJA. Use of the International Convention on Service Abroad of Judicial and Extrajudicial Documents (T.I.A.S. 6638, 20 U.S.T. 361; see anno. to F.R. civ. P. 4(i) in 28 U.S.C.A.)—an almost laughable example of the continental European mind's fascination with bureaucratic redundancies—is a prospect filled with uncertainty. The U.S. Marshals Service, explaining its facilitation of Convention service in DOJ Memo. No. 386, portrays a system in which service can be very uncertain, and agonizingly delayed by foreign officials. The problem lies in the substantial possibility that any minor child is likely to have reached his majority, and any litigating parent to have reached bankruptcy, by the time service is effected and proved under that document in a domestic relations case. Whether it is mandatory is another large question. Courts have taken the position that the Convention simply provides a convenient alternative to whatever means of foreign-country service state law provides, including service by mail (*Tamari v. Bache & Co.*, 431 F.Supp. 1226, 1228 (N.D. Ill. 1977); *Shoei Kako Co. v. Super. Ct.*, 33 Cal. App. 3d 808, 821 (1973); *Int'l Controls Corp. v. Vesco.*, 593 F2d 166, 179 (CA2, 1979)). But many individual foreign countries have signed with reservations against allowing postal and other kinds of service. Also the State Department, encouraged by the protest notes and by such cases as *Kadota v. Hosogai*, 608 P.2d 68 (Ariz. 1980), and *FTC v. Compagnie de St. Gobain-Pont a Mousson*, 636 F.2d, 1300, 49 LW 2362 (CADC, 11/17/80) (involving service on *foreign* nationals in their own lands), has been using all the means at its disposal to get stateside plaintiffs to use the Convention exclusively. If the Convention is regarded as the exclusive means of service, then the question whether it prevails over UCCJA Section 5 would seem to be answered by the "law of the land" clause of the U.S. Constitution's Article VI, making federal statutes and treaties previal over inconsistent state law. However, the UCCJA petitioner's attorney, and the judge he is trying to please, are likely to look only at Section 5 when assessing the legal sufficiency of service to make a given UCCJA claim entertainable in an American state trial court. After the American judge is pleased, the service had and the case entertained, the State Department view of Convention exclusivity may arise only upon a later special appearance or on appeal, if at all.

Constitutional challenges to the UCCJA have doubtless been around nearly as long as the statute itself, seldom rising above the trial court level.

However they have been given something of a new dimension by the rulings in *Kulko v. Superior Court,* 436 U.S. 84, 4 FLR 3075 (1978), and the *Shaffer v. Heitner,* 433 U.S. 186 (1978), opinion on which it was based. As noted earlier, *Shaffer* held, that there was no more "quasi in rem" jurisdiction theory, since personal jurisdiction minimum contacts of the "International Shoe" sort (see *International Shoe Co. Inc. v. Washington,* 326 U.S. 310 (1945)) have to be present for quasi in rem jurisdiction also—thus leaving little of the classical theory of "divisible divorce" that is not in doubt. The Georgia Supreme Court had no trouble turning aside constitutional challenges in *Goldfarb v. Goldfarb,* 268 S.E. 2d 648, 6 FLR 2637 (1980), and *Yearta v. Scroggins,* 268 S.E.2d 151, 6 FLR 2644 (1980), by analyzing the old U.S. Supreme Court custody jurisdiction cases from before *Shaffer* and *Kulko. Giddings v. Giddings,* 228 N.W.2d 915 (N.D. 1975), hinted at a constitutional issue, but did not reach it in that case.

In any event, getting a federal court to accept jurisdiction over any UCCJA case, even by bringing a federal constitutional challenge to the Uniform Act, may be difficult in view of the long-standing "domestic relations exception" to federal jurisdiction which dates at least from *Barber v. Barber,* 62 U.S. 582 (1859). See *Eramo v. Eramo,* F.Supp. 7 FLR 2207 (N.D.N.Y. 12/31/80), for a lengthy discussion of the exception and a refusal to open the federal courts to such a claim.

However, what effect the Wallop Amendment will have on this long-lived allocation of federal and state jurisdiction is hard to say. Though the theory of the Wallop Amendment's foundation of federal power to dictate custody law to the states' courts is unclear to say the least, the possibility certainly exists that challenges to a state's failure or refusal to abide by what a party perceives as the requirements of the Wallop Amendment will have to come ultimately to a federal court. Whether this will end up appearing as a state-versus-state lawsuit under the U.S. Supreme Court's original jurisdiction, or whether there will have to be further amendments to Title 28 of the U.S. Code to allow a new basis for citizens suits against sovereign states remains to be seen and is a fertile field for scholarly inquiry.

# FULL OFFICIAL TEXT OF ACT, WITH COMMENTARY

*Reproduced by permission of the National Conference of Commissioners on Uniform State Laws*

## Uniform Child Custody Jurisdiction Act

### Prefatory Note

There is growing public concern over the fact that thousands of children are shifted from state to state and from one family to another every year while their parents or other persons battle over their custody in the courts of several states. Children of separated parents may live with their mother, for example, but one day the father snatches them and brings them to another state where he petitions a court to award him custody while the mother starts custody proceedings in her state; or in the case of illness of the mother the children may be cared for by grandparents in a third state, and all three parties may fight over the right to keep the children in several states. These and many similar situations constantly arise in our mobile society where family members often are scattered all over the United States and at times over other countries. A young child may have been moved to another state repeatedly before the case goes to court. When a decree has been rendered awarding custody to one of the parties, this is by no means the end of the child's migrations. It is well known that those who lose a court battle over custody are often unwilling to accept the judgment of the court. They will remove the child in an unguarded moment or fail to return him after a visit and will seek their luck in the court of a distant state where they hope to find—and often do find—a more sympathetic ear for their plea for custody. The party deprived of the child may then resort to similar tactics to recover the child and this "game" may continue for years, with the child thrown back and forth from state to state, never coming to rest in one single home and in one community.

The harm done to children by these experiences can hardly be overestimated. It does not require an expert in the behavioral sciences to know that a child, especially during his early years and the years of growth, needs security and stability of environment and a continuity of affection. A child who has never been given the chance to develop a sense of belonging and whose personal attachments when beginning to form are cruelly disrupted, may well be crippled for life, to his own lasting detriment and the detriment of society.

This unfortunate state of affairs has been aided and facilitated rather than discouraged by the law. There is no statutory law in this area and the judicial law is so unsettled that it seems to offer nothing but a "quicksand foundation" to stand on. See Leflar, American Conflicts Law 585 (1968). See also Clark, Domestic Relations 320 (1968). There is no certainty as to which state has jurisdiction when persons seeking custody of a child approach the courts of several states simultaneously or successively. There is no certainty as to whether a custody decree rendered in one state is entitled to recognition and enforcement in another; nor as to when one state may alter a custody decree of a sister state.

The judicial trend has been toward permitting custody claimants to sue in the courts of almost any state, no matter how fleeting the contact of the child and family was with the particular state, with little regard to any conflict of law rules. See Leflar, American Conflicts Law 585-6 (1968) and Leflar, 1967 Annual Survey of American Law, Conflict of Laws 26 (1968). Also, since the United States Supreme Court has never settled the question whether the full faith and credit clause of the Constitution applies to custody decrees, many states have felt free to modify custody decrees of sister states almost at random although the theory usually is that there has been a change of circumstances requiring a custody award to a different person. Compare *People ex rel. Halvey v. Halvey,* 330 U.S. 610, 67 S. Ct. 903, 91 L. Ed. 1133 (1947); and see Comment, Ford v. Ford: Full Faith and Credit To Child Custody Decrees? 73 Yale L. J. 134 (1963). Generally speaking, there has been a tendency to over-emphasize the need for fluidity and modifiability of custody decrees at the expense of the equal (if not greater) need, from the standpoint of the child, for stability of custody decisions once made. Compare Clark, Domestic Relations 326 (1968).

Under this state of the law the courts of the various states have acted in isolation and at times in competition with each other; often with disastrous consequences. A court of one state may have awarded custody to the mother while another state decreed simultaneously that the child must go to the father. See *Stout v. Pate,* 209 Ga. 786, 75 S.E. 2d 748 (1953) and *Stout v. Pate,* 120 Cal. App. 2d 699, 261 P. 2d 788 (1953), cert. denied in both cases 347 U.S. 968, 74 S. Ct. 744, 776, 98 L. Ed. 1109, 1110 (1954); *Moniz v. Moniz,* 142 Cal. App. 2d 527, 298 P. 2d 710 (1956); and *Sharpe v. Sharpe,* 77 Ill. App. 2d 295, 222 N.E. 2d 340 (1966). In situations like this the litigants do not know which court to obey. They may face punishment for contempt of court and perhaps criminal charges for child stealing in one state when complying with the decree of the other. Also, a custody decree made in one state one year is often overturned in another jurisdiction the next year or some years later and the child is handed over to another family, to be repeated as long as the feud continues. See *Com. ex rel. Thomas v.*

*Gillard,* 203 Pa. Super. 95, 198 A 2d 377 (1964); *In Re Guardianship of Rodgers,* 100 Ariz. 269, 413 P. 2d 774 (1966); *Berlin v. Berlin,* 239 Md. 52, 210 A. 2d 380 (1965); *Berlin v. Berlin,* 21 N.Y. 2d 371, 235 N.E. 2d 109 (1967), cert. denied 37 L.W. 3123 (1968); and *Batchelor v. Fulcher,* 415 S.W. 2d 828 (Ky. 1967).

In this confused legal situation the person who has possession of the child has an enormous tactical advantage. Physical presence of the child opens the doors of many courts to the petitions and often assures him of a decision in his favor. It is not surprising then that custody claimants tend to take the law into their own hands, that they resort to self-help in the form of child stealing, kidnapping, or various other schemes to gain possession of the child. The irony is that persons who are good, law-abiding citizens are often driven into these tactics against their inclinations; and that lawyers who are reluctant to advise the use of maneuver of doubtful legality may place their clients at a decided disadvantage.

To remedy this intolerable state of affairs where self-help and the rule of "seize-and-run" prevail rather than the orderly processes of the law, uniform legislation has been urged in recent years to bring about a fair measure of interstate stability in custody awards. See Ratner, Child Custody in a Federal System, 62 Mich. L. Rev. 795 (1964); Ratner, Legislative Resolution of the Interstate Child Custody Problem: A Reply to Professor Currie and a Proposed Uniform Act, 38 S. Cal. L. Rev. 183 (1965); and Ehrenzweig, The Interstate Child and Uniform Legislation: A Plea for Extra-Litigious Proceedings, 64 Mich. L. Rev. 1 (1965). In drafting this Act, the National Conference of Commissioners has drawn heavily on the work of these authors and has consulted with other leading authorities in the field. The American Bar Association has taken an active part in furthering the project.

The Act is designed to bring some semblence of order into the existing chaos. It limits custody jurisdiction to the state where the child has his home or where there are other strong contacts with the child and his family. See Section 3. It provides for the recognition and enforcement of out-of-state custody decrees in many instances. See Sections 13 and 15. Jurisdiction to modify decrees of other states is limited by giving a jurisdictional preference to the prior court under certain conditions. See Section 14. Access to a court may be denied to petitioners who have engaged in child snatching or similar practices. See Section 8. Also, the Act opens up direct lines of communication between courts of different states to prevent jurisdictional conflict and bring about interstate judicial assistance in custody cases.

The Act stresses the importance of the personal appearance before the court of non-residents who claim custody, and of the child himself, and provides for the payment of travel expenses for this purpose. See

Section 11. Further provisions insure that the judge receives necessary out-of-state information with the assistance of courts in other states. See Sections 17 through 22.

Underlying the entire Act is the idea that to avoid the jurisdictional conflicts and confusions which have done serious harm to innumerable children, a court in one state must assume major responsibility to determine who is to have custody of a particular child; that this court must reach out for the help of courts in other states in order to arrive at a fully informed judgment which transcends state lines and considers all claimants, residents and nonresidents, on an equal basis and from the standpoint of the welfare of the child. If this can be achieved, it will be less important *which* court exercises jurisdiction but that courts of the several states involved act in partnership to bring about the best possible solution for a child's future.

The Act is not a reciprocal law. It can be put into full operation by each individual state regardless of enactment of other states. But its full benefits will not be reaped until a large number of states have enacted it, and until the courts, perhaps aided by regional or national conferences, have come to develop a new, truly "inter-state" approach to child custody litigation. The general policies of the Act and some of its specific provisions apply to international custody cases.

## Uniform Child Custody Jurisdiction Act

**Section 1.** [*Purposes of Act; Contruction of Provisions.*]

(a) The general purposes of this Act are to:

(1) avoid jurisdictional competition and conflict with courts of other states in matters of child custody which have in the past resulted in the shifting of children from state to state with harmful effects on their well-being;

(2) promote cooperation with the courts of other states to the end that a custody decree is rendered in that state which can best decide the case in the interest of the child;

(3) assure that litigation concerning the custody of a child take place ordinarily in the state with which the child and his family have the closest connection and where significant evidence concerning his care, protection, training, and personal relationships is most readily available, and that courts of this state decline the exercise of jurisdiction when the child and his family have a closer connection with another state;

(4) discourage continuing controversies over child custody in the interest of greater stability of home environment and of secure family relationships for the child;

(5) deter abductions and other unilateral removals of children undertaken to obtain custody awards;

(6) avoid re-litigation of custody decisions of other states in this state insofar as feasible;

(7) facilitate the enforcement of custody decrees of other states;

(8) promote and expand the exchange of information and other forms of mutual assistance between the courts of this state and those of other states concerned with the same child; and

(9) make uniform the law of those states which enact it.

(b) This Act shall be construed to promote the general purposes stated in this section.

### Comment

Because this uniform law breaks new ground not previously covered by legislation, its purposes are stated in some detail. Each section must be read and applied with these purposes in mind.

SECTION 2. [*Definitions.*] As used in this Act:

(1) "contestant" means a person, including a parent, who claims a right to custody or visitation rights with respect to a child;

(2) "custody determination" means a court decision and court orders and instructions providing for the custody of a child, including visitation rights; it does not include a decision relating to child support or any other monetary obligation of any person;

(3) "custody proceeding" includes proceedings in which a custody determination is one of several issues, such as an action for divorce or separation, and includes child neglect and dependency proceedings;

(4) "decree" or "custody decree" means a custody determination contained in a judicial decree or order made in a custody proceeding, and includes an initial decree and a modification decree;

(5) "home state" means the state in which the child immediately preceding the time involved lived with his parents, a parent, or a person acting as parent, for at least 6 consecutive months, and in the case of a child less than 6 months old the state in which the child lived from birth with any of the persons mentioned. Periods of temporary absence of any of the named persons are counted as part of the 6-month or other period;

(6) "initial decree" means the first custody decree concerning a particular child;

(7) "modification decree" means a custody decree which modifies or replaces a prior decree, whether made by the court which rendered the prior decree or by another court;

(8) "physical custody" means actual possession and control of a child;

(9) "person acting as parent" means a person, other than a parent, who has physical custody of a child and who has either been awarded custody by a court or claims a right to custody; and

(10) "state" means any state, territory, or possession of the United States, the Commonweath of Puerto Rico, and the District of Columbia.

### COMMENT

Subsection (3) indicates that "custody proceeding" is to be understood in a broad sense. The term covers habeas corpus actions, guardianship petitions, and other proceedings available under general state law to determine custody. See Clark, Domestic Relations 576-582 (1968).

Other definitions are explained, if necessary, in the comments to the sections which use the terms defined.

SECTION 3. [*Jurisdiction.*]

(a) A court of this State which is competent to decide child custody matters has jurisdiction to make a child custody determination by initial or modification decree if:

(1) this State (i) is the home state of the child at the time of commencement of the proceeding, or (ii) had been the child's home state within 6 months before commencement of the proceeding and the child is absent from this State because of his removal or retention by a person claiming his custody or for other reasons, and a parent or person acting as parent continues to live in this State; or

(2) it is in the best interest of the child that a court of this State assume jurisdiction because (i) the child and his parents, or the child and at least one contestant, have a significant connection with this State, and (ii) there is available in this State substantial evidence concerning the child's present or future care, protection, training, and personal relationships; or

(3) the child is physically present in this State and (i) the child has been abandoned or (ii) it is necessary in an emergency to protect the child because he has been subjected to or threatened with mistreatment or abuse or is otherwise neglected [or dependent]; or

(4) (i) it appears that no other state would have jurisdiction under prerequisites substantially in accordance with paragraphs (1), (2), or (3), or another state has declined to exercise jurisdiction on the ground that this State is the more appropriate forum to determine the custody of the child, and (ii) it is in the best interest of the child that this court assume jurisdiction.

(b) Except under paragraphs (3) and (4) of subsection (a), physical presence in this State of the child, or of the child and one of the contestants, is not alone sufficient to confer jurisdiction on a court of this State to make a child custody determination.

(c) Physical presence of the child, while desirable, is not a prerequisite for jurisdiction to determine his custody.

### COMMENT

Paragraphs (1) and (2) of subsection (a) establish the two major bases for jurisdiction. In the first place, a court in the child's home state has jurisdiction, and secondly, if there is no home state or the child and his family have equal or stronger ties with another state, a court in that state has jurisdiction. If this alternative test produces concurrent jurisdiction in more than one state, the mechanisms provided in sections 6 and 7 are used to assure that only one state makes the custody decision.

"Home state" is defined in section 2(5). A 6-month period has been selected in order to have a definite and certain test which is at the same time based on a reasonable assumption of fact. See Ratner, Child Custody in a Federal System, 62 Mich. L. Rev. 795, 818 (1964) who explains:

> "Most American children are integrated into an American community after living there six months; consequently this period of residence would seem to provide a reasonable criterion for identifying the established home."

Subparagraph (ii) of paragraph (1) extends the home state rule for an additional six-month period in order to permit suit in the home state after the child's departure. The main objective is to protect a parent who has been left by his spouse taking the child along. The provision makes clear that the stay-at-home parent, if he acts promptly, may start proceedings in his own state if he desires, without the necessity of attempting to base jurisdiction on paragraph (2). This changes the law in those states which required presence of the child as a condition for jurisdiction and consequently forced the person left behind to follow the departed person to another state, perhaps to several states in succession. See also subsection (c).

Paragraph (2) comes into play either when the home state test cannot be met or as an alternative to that test. The first situation arises, for example, when a family has moved frequently and there is no state where the child has lived for 6 months prior to suit, or if the child has recently been removed from his home state and the person who was left behind has also moved away. See paragraph (1), last clause. A typical example of alternative jurisdiction is the case in which the stay-at-home parent chooses to follow the departed spouse to state 2 (where the child has lived for several months with the other parent) and starts proceedings there. Whether the departed parent also has access to a court in state 2, depends on the strength of the family ties in that state and on the applicability of the clean hands provision of section 8. If state 2, for example, was the state of the matrimonial home where the entire family lived for two years before moving to the "home state" for 6 months, and the wife returned to state 2 with the child with the consent of the husband, state 2 might well have jurisdiction upon petition of the wife. The same may be true if the wife returned to her parents in her former home state where the child had spent several months every year before. Compare Willmore v. Willmore, 273, Minn. 537, 143 N.W. 2d 630 (1966), cert. denied 385 U.S. 898 (1966). While jurisdiction may exist in two states in these instances, it will not be *exercised* in both states. See sections 6 and 7.

Paragraph (2) of subsection (a) is supplemented by subsection (b) which is designed to discourage unilateral removal of children to other states and to guard generally against too liberal an interpretation of paragraph (2). Short-term presence in the state is not enough even though there may be an intent to stay longer, perhaps an intent to establish a technical "domicile" for divorce or other purposes.

Paragraph (2) perhaps more than any other provision of the Act requires that it be interpreted in the spirit of the legislative purposes expressed in section 1. The paragraph was phrased in general terms in order to be flexible enough to cover many fact situations too diverse to lend themselves to exact description. But its purpose is to limit jurisdiction rather than to proliferate it. The first clause of the paragraph is important: jurisdiction exists only if it is in the *child's* interest, not merely the interest or convenience of the feuding parties, to determine custody in a particular state. The interest of the child is served when the forum has optimum access to relevant evidence about the child and family. There must be maximum rather than minimum contact with the state. The submission of the parties to a forum, perhaps for purposes of divorce, is not sufficient without additional factors establishing closer ties with the state. Divorce jurisdiction does not necessarily include custody jurisdiction. See Clark, Domestic Relations 578 (1968).

Paragraph (3) of subsection (a) retains and reaffirms *parens patriae* jurisdiction, usually exercised by a juvenile court, which a state must assume when a child is in a situation requiring immediate protection. This jurisdiction exists when a child has been abandoned and in emergency cases of child neglect. Presence of the child in the state is the only prerequisite. This extraordinary jurisdiction is reserved for extraordinary circumstances. See Application of Lang, 9 App. Div. 2d 401, 193 N.Y.S. 2d 763 (1959). When there is child neglect without emergency or abandonment, jurisdiction cannot be based on this paragraph.

Paragraph (4) of subsection (a) provides a final basis for jurisdiction which is subsidiary in nature. It is to be resorted to only if no other state could, or would, assume jurisdiction under the other criteria of this section.

Subsection (c) makes it clear that presence of the child is not a jurisdictional requirement. Subseqent sections are designed to assure the appearance of the child before the court.

This section governs jurisdiction to make an initial decree as well as a modification decree. Both terms are defined in section 2. Jurisdiction to modify an initial or modification decree of another state is subject to additional restrictions contained in sections 8(b) and 14(a).

SECTION 4. [*Notice and Opportunity to be Heard.*] Before making a decree under this Act, reasonable notice and opportunity to be heard shall be given to the contestants, any parent whose parental rights have not been previously terminated, and any person who has physical custody of the child. If any of these persons is outside this State, notice and opportunity to be heard shall be given pursuant to section 5.

COMMENT

This section lists the persons who must be notified and given an opportunity to be heard to satisfy due process requirements. As to persons in the forum state, the general law of the state applies; others are notified in accordance with section 5. Strict compliance with sections 4 and 5 is essential for the validity of a custody decree within the state and its recognition and enforcement in other states under sections 12, 13, and 15. See Restatement of the Law Second, Conflict of Laws, Proposed Official Draft sec. 69 (1967); and compare Armstrong v. Manzo, 380 U.S. 545, 85 S. Ct. 1187, 14 L. Ed. 2d 62 (1965).

SECTION 5. [*Notice to Persons Outside this State; Submission to Jurisdiction.*]

(a) Notice required for the exercise of jurisdiction over a person outside this State shall be given in a manner reasonably calculated to give actual notice, and may be:

(1) by personal delivery outside this State in the manner prescribed for service of process within this State;

(2) in the manner prescribed by the law of the place in which the service is made for service of process in that place in an action in any of its courts of general jurisdiction;

(3) by any form of mail addressed to the person to be served and requesting a receipt; or

(4) as directed by the court [including publication, if other means of notification are ineffective].

(b) Notice under this section shall be served, mailed, or delivered, [or last published] at least [10, 20] days before any hearing in this State.

(c) Proof of service outside this State may be made by affidavit of the individual who made the service, or in the manner prescribed by the law of this State, the order pursuant to which the service is made, or the law of the place in which the service is made. If service is made by mail, proof may be a receipt signed by the addressee or other evidence of delivery to the addressee.

(d) Notice is not required if a person submits to the jurisdiction of the court.

### Comment

Section 2.01 of the Uniform Interstate and International Procedure Act has been followed to a large extent. See 9B U.L.A. 315 (1966). If at all possible, actual notice should be received by the affected persons; but efforts to impart notice in a manner reasonably calculated to give actual notice are sufficient when a person who may perhaps conceal his whereabouts, cannot be reached. See Mullane v. Central Hanover Bank and Trust Co., 339 U.S. 306, 70 S. Ct. 652, 94 L. Ed. 865 (1950) and Schroeder v. City of New York, 371 U.S. 208, 83 S. Ct. 279, 9 L. Ed. 2d 255 (1962).

Notice by publication in lieu of other means of notification is not included because of its doubtful constitutionality. See Mullane v. Central Hanover Bank and Trust Co., *supra;* and see Hazard, A General Theory of State-Court Jurisdiction, 1965 Supreme Court Rev. 241, 277, 286-87. Paragraph (4) of subsection (a) lists notice by publication in brackets for the benefit of those states which desire to use published notices *in addition to* the modes of notification provided in this section when these modes prove ineffective to impart actual notice.

The provisions of this section, and paragraphs (2) and (4) of subsection (a) in particular, are subject to the caveat that notice and opportunity to be heard must always meet due process requirements as they exist at the time of the proceeding.

SECTION 6. [*Simultaneous Proceedings in Other States.*]

(a) A court of this State shall not exercise its jurisdiction under this Act if at the time of filing the petition a proceeding concerning the custody of the child was pending in a court of another state exercising jurisdiction substantially in conformity with this Act, unless the proceeding is stayed by the court of the other state because this State is a more appropriate forum or for other reasons.

(b) Before hearing the petition in a custody proceeding the court shall examine the pleadings and other information supplied by the parties under section 9 and shall consult the child custody registry established under section 16 concerning the pendency of proceedings with respect to the child in other states. If the court has reason to believe that proceedings may be pending in another state it shall direct an inquiry to the state court administrator or other appropriate official of the other state.

(c) If the court is informed during the course of the proceeding that a proceeding concerning the custody of the child was pending in another state before the court assumed jurisdiction it shall stay the proceeding and communicate with the court in which the other proceeding is pending to the end that the issue may be litigated in the more appropriate forum and that information be exchanged in accordance with sections 19 through 22. If a court of this state has made a custody decree before being informed of a pending proceeding in a court of another state it shall immediately inform that court of the fact. If the court is informed that a proceeding was commenced in another state after it assumed jurisdiction it shall likewise inform the other court to the end that the issues may be litigated in the more appropriate forum.

### Comment

Because of the havoc wreaked by simultaneous and competitive jurisdiction which has been described in the Prefatory Note, this section seeks to avoid jurisdictional conflict with all feasible means, including novel methods. Courts are expected to take an active part under this section in seeking out information about custody proceedings concerning the same child pending in other states. In a proper case jurisdiction is yielded to the other state either under this section or under section 7. Both sections must be read together.

When the courts of more than one state have jurisdiction under sections 3 or 14, priority in time determines which court will proceed with the action, but the application of the inconvenient forum principle of section 7 may result in the handling of the case by the other court.

While jurisdiction need not be yielded under subsection (a) if the other court would not have jurisdiction under the criteria of this Act, the policy against simultaneous custody proceedings is so strong that it might in a particular situation be appropriate to leave the case to the other court even under such circumstances. See subsection (3) and section 7.

Once a custody decree has been rendered in one state, jurisdiction is determined by sections 8 and 14.

Section 7. [*Inconvenient Forum.*]

(a) A court which has jurisdiction under this Act to make an initial or modification decree may decline to exercise its jurisdiction any time before making a decree if it finds that it is an inconvenient forum to make a custody determination under the circumstances of the case and that a court of another state is a more appropriate forum.

(b) A finding of inconvenient forum may be made upon the

court's own motion or upon motion of a party or a guardian ad litem or other representative of the child.

(c) In determining if it is an inconvenient forum, the court shall consider if it is in the interest of the child that another state assume jurisdiction. For this purpose it may take into account the following factors, among others:

(1) if another state is or recently was the child's home state;

(2) if another state has a closer connection with the child and his family or with the child and one or more of the contestants;

(3) if substantial evidence concerning the child's present or future care, protection, training, and personal relationships is more readily available in another state;

(4) if the parties have agreed on another forum which is no less appropriate; and

(5) if the exercise of jurisdiction by a court of this state would contravene any of the purposes stated in section 1.

(d) Before determing whether to decline or retain jurisdiction the court may communicate with a court of another state and exchange information pertinent to the assumption of jurisdiction by either court with a view to assuring that jurisdiction will be exercised by the more appropriate court and that a forum will be available to the parties.

(e) If the court finds that it is an inconvenient forum and that a court of another state is a more appropriate forum, it may dismiss the proceedings, or it may stay the proceedings upon condition that a custody proceeding be promptly commenced in another named state or upon any other conditions which may be just and proper, including the condition that a moving party stipulate his consent and submission to the jurisdiction of the other forum.

(f) The court may decline to exercise its jurisdiction under this Act if a custody determination is incidental to an action for divorce or another proceeding while retaining jurisdiction over the divorce or other proceeding.

(g) If it appears to the court that it is clearly an inappropriate forum it may require the party who commenced the proceedings to pay, in addition to the costs of the proceedings in this State, necessary travel and other expenses, including attorneys' fees, incurred by other parties or their witnesses. Payment is to be made to the clerk of the court for remittance to the proper party.

(h) Upon dismissal or stay of proceedings under this section the court shall inform the court found to be the more appropriate forum of this fact, of if the court which would have jurisdiction in the other state is not certainly known, shall transmit the information to the court administrator or other appropriate official for forwarding to the appropriate court.

(i) Any communication received from another state informing this State of a finding of inconvenient forum because a court of this State is the more appropriate forum shall be filed in the custody registry of the appropriate court. Upon assuming jurisdiction the court of this State shall inform the original court of this fact.

### COMMENT

The purpose of this provision is to encourage judicial restraint in exercising jurisdiction whenever another state appears to be in a better position to determine custody of a child. It serves as a second check on jurisdiction once the test of sections 3 or 14 has been met.

The section is a particular application of the inconvenient forum principle, recognized in most states by judicial law, adapted to the special needs of child custody cases. The terminology used follows section 84 of the Restatement of the Law Second, Conflict of Laws, Proposed Official Draft (1967). Judicial restrictions or exceptions to the inconvenient forum rule made in some states do not apply to this statutory scheme which is limited to child custody cases.

Like section 6, this section stresses interstate judicial communication and cooperation. When there is doubt as to which is the more appropriate forum, the question may be resolved by consultation and cooperation among the courts involved.

Paragraphs (1) through (5) of subsection (c) specify some, but not all, considerations which enter into a court determination of inconvenient forum. Factors customarily listed for purposes of the general principle of the inconvenient forum (such as convenience of the parties and hardship to the defendant) are also pertinent, but may under the circumstances be of secondary importance because the child who is not a party is the central figure in the proceedings.

Part of subsection (e) is derived from Wis. Stat. Ann., sec. 262.19 (1).

Subsection (f) makes it clear that a court may divide a case, that is, dismiss part of it and retain the rest. See section 1.05 of the Uniform Interstate and International Procedure Act. When the custody issue comes up in a divorce proceeding, courts may have frequent occasion to decline jurisdiction as to that issue (assuming that custody jurisdiction exists under sections 3 or 14).

Subsection (g) is an adaptation of Wis. Stat. Ann., sec. 262.20 Its purpose is to serve as a deterrent against "frivolous jurisdiction claims," as G.W. Foster states in the Revision Notes to the Wisconsin provision. It applies when the forum chosen is seriously inappropriate considering the jurisdictional requirements of the Act.

SECTION 8. [*Jurisdiction Declined by Reason of Conduct.*]

(a) If the petitioner for an initial decree has wrongfully taken the child from another state or has engaged in similar reprehensible conduct the court may decline to exercise jurisdiction if this is just and proper under the circumstances.

(b) Unless required in the interest of the child, the court shall not exercise its jurisdiction to modify a custody decree of another state if the petitioner, without consent of the person entitled to custody, has improperly removed the child from the physical custody of the person entitled to custody or has improperly retained the child after a visit or other temporary relinquishment of physical custody. If the petitioner has violated any other provision of a custody decree of another state the court may decline to exercise its jurisdiction if this is just and proper under the circumstances.

(c) In appropriate cases a court dismissing a petition under this section may charge the petitioner with necessary travel and other expenses, including attorneys' fees, incurred by other parties or their witnesses.

### COMMENT

This section incorporates the "clean hands doctrine," so named by Ehrenzweig, Interstate Recognition of Custody Decrees, 51 Mich. L. Rev. 345 (1953). Under this doctrine courts refuse to assume jurisdiction to reexamine an out-of-state custody decree when the petitioner has abducted the child or has engaged in some other objectionable scheme to gain or retain physical custody of the child in violation of the decree. See Fain, Custody of Children, The California Family Lawyer I, 539, 546 (1961); Ex Parte Mullins, 26 Wash. 2d 419, 174 P. 2d 790 (1946); Crocker v. Crocker, 122 Colo. 49, 219 P. 2d 311 (1950); and Leathers v. Leathers, 162 Cal. App. 2d 768, 328 P. 2d 853 (1958). But when adherence to this rule would lead to punishment of the parent at the expense of the wellbeing of the child, it is often not applied. See Smith v. Smith, 135 Cal. App. 2d 100, 286 P. 2d 1009 (1955) and In re Guardianship of Rodgers, 100 Ariz. 269, 413 P. 2d 744 (1966).

Subsection (a) extends the clean hands principle to cases in which a custody decree has not yet been rendered in any state. For example, if upon a de facto separation the wife returned to her own home with the children without objection by her husband and lived there for two years without hearing from him, and the husband without warning forcibly removes the children one night and brings them to another state, a court in that state although it has jurisdiction after 6 months may decline to hear the huband's custody petition. "Wrongfully" taking under this subsection does not mean that a "right" has been violated-both husband and wife as a rule have a right to custody until a court determination is made-but that one party's conduct is so objectionable that a court in the exercise of its inherent equity powers cannot in good conscience permit that party access to its jurisdiction.

Subsection (b) does not come into operation unless the court has power under section 14 to modify the custody decree of another state. It is a codification of the clean hands rule, except that it differentiates between (1) a taking or retention of the child and (2) other violations of custody decrees. In the case of illegal removal or retention refusal of jursdiction is mandatory unless the harm done to the child by a denial of jurisdiction outweighs the parental misconduct. Compare Smith v. Smith and In Re Guardianship of Rodgers, *supra;* and see In Re Walter, 228 Cal. App. 2d 217, 39 Cal. Rpts. 243 (1964) where the court assumed jurisdiction after both parents had been guilty of misconduct. The qualifying word "improperly" is added to exclude cases in which a child is withheld because of illness or other emergency or in which there are other special justifying circumstances.

The most common violation of the second category is the removal of the child from the state by the parent who has the right to custody, thereby frustrating the exercise of visitation rights of the other parent. The second sentence of subsection

(b) makes refusal of jurisdiction entirely discretionary in this situation because it depends on the circumstances whether non-compliance with the court order is serious enough to warrant the drastic sanction of denial of jurisdiction.

Subsection (c) adds a financial deterrent to child stealing and similar reprehensible conduct.

SECTION 9. [*Information under Oath to be Submitted to the Court.*]

(a) Every party in a custody proceeding in his first pleading or in an affidavit attached to that pleading shall give information under oath as to the child's present address, the places where the child has lived within the last 5 years, and the names and present addresses of the persons with whom the child has lived during that period. In this pleading or affidavit every party shall further declare under oath whether:

(1) he has participated (as a party, witness, or in any other capacity) in any other litigation concerning the custody of the same child in this or any other state;

(2) he has information of any custody proceeding concerning the child pending in a court of this or any other state; and

(3) he knows of any person not a party to the proceedings who has physical custody of the child or claims to have custody or visitation rights with respect to the child.

(b) If the declaration as to any of the above items is in the affirmative the declarant shall give additional information under oath as required by the court. The court may examine the parties under oath as to details of the information furnished and as to other matters pertinent to the court's jurisdiction and the disposition of the case.

(c) Each party has a continuing duty to inform the court of any custody proceeding concerning the child in this or any other state of which he obtained information during this proceeding.

COMMENT

It is important for the court to receive the information listed and other pertinent facts as early as possible for purposes of determining its jurisdiction, the joinder of additional parties, and the identification of courts in other states which are to be contacted under various provisions of the Act. Information as to custody litigation and other pertinent facts occurring in other countries may also be elicited under this section in combination with section 23.

SECTION 10. [*Additional Parties.*] If the court learns from information furnished by the parties pursuant to section 9 or from other sources that a person not a party to the custody proceeding has physical custody of the child or claims to have custody or visitation rights with respect to the child, it shall order that person to be joined as a party and to be duly notified of the pendency of the proceeding and of his joinder as a party. If the person joined as a party is outside this State he shall be served with process or otherwise notified in accordance with section 5.

COMMENT

The purpose of this section is to prevent re-litigations of the custody issue when these would be for the benefit of third claimants rather than the child. If the immediate controversy, for example, is between the parents, but relatives inside or outside the state also claim custody or have physical custody which may lead to a future claim to the child, they must be brought into the proceedings. The courts are given an active role here as under other sections of the Act to seek out the necessary information from formal or informal sources.

SECTION 11. [*Appearance of Parties and the Child.*]

[(a) The court may order any party to the proceeding who is in this State to appear personally before the court. If that party has physical custody of the child the court may order that he appear personally with the child.]

(b) If a party to the proceeding whose presence is desired by the court is outside this State with or without the child the court may order that the notice given under section 5 include a statement directing that party to appear personally with or without the child and declaring that failure to appear may result in a decision adverse to that party.

(c) If a party to the proceeding who is outside this State is directed to appear under subsection (b) or desires to appear personally before the court with or without the child, the court may require another party to pay to the clerk of the court travel and other necessary expenses of the party so appearing and of the child if this is just and proper under the circumstances.

COMMENT

Since a custody proceeding is concerned with the past and future care of the child by one of the parties, it is of vital importance in most cases that the judge has an opportunity to see and hear the contestants and the child. Subsection (a) authorizes the court to order the appearance of these persons if they are in the state. It is placed in brackets because states which have such a provision—not only in their juvenile court laws—may wish to omit it. Subsection (b) relates to the appearance of persons who are outside the state and provides one method of bringing them before the court; sections 19(b) and 20(b) provide another. Subsection (c) helps to finance travel to the court which may be close to one of the parties and distant from another; it may be used to equalize the expense if this is appropriate under the circumstances.

SECTION 12. [*Binding Force and Res Judicata Effect of Custody Decree.*] A custody decree rendered by a court of this State which had jurisdiction under section 3 binds all parties who have been served in this State or notified in accordance with section 5 or who have submitted to the jurisdiction of the court, and who have been given an opportunity to be heard. As to these parties the custody decree is conclusive as to all issues of law and fact decided and as to the custody determination made unless and until that determination is modified pursuant to law, including the provisions of this Act.

### COMMENT

This section deals with the intra-state validity of custody decrees which provides the basis for their interstate recognition and enforcement. The two prerequisites are (1) jurisdiction under section 3 of this Act and (2) strict compliance with due process mandates of notice and opportunity to be heard. There is no requirement for technical personal jurisdiction, on the traditional theory that custody determinations, as distinguished from support actions (see section 2(2) *supra*), are proceedings in rem or proceedings affecting status. See Restatement of the Law Second, Conflict of Laws, Proposed Official Draft, sections 69 and 79 (1967); and James, Civil Procedure 613 (1965). For a different theory reaching the same result, see Hazard, A General Theory of State-Court Jurisdiction, 1965 Supreme Court Review 241. The section is not at variance with May v. Anderson, 345 U.S. 528, 73 S. Ct. 840, 97 L. Ed. 1221 (1953), which relates to interstate recognition rather than in-state validity of custody decrees. See Ehrenzweig and Louisell, Jurisdiction in a Nutshell 76 (2d ed. 1968); and compare Reese, Full Faith and Credit to Foreign Equity Decrees, 42 Iowa L. Rev. 183, 195 (1957). On May v. Anderson, *supra*, see comment to section 13.

Since a custody decree is nomally subject to modification in the interest of the child, it does not have absolute finality, but as long as it has not been modified, it is as binding as a final judgment. Compare Restatement of the Law Second, Conflict of Laws, Proposed Official Draft, section 109 (1967).

SECTION 13. [*Recognition of Out-of-State Custody Decrees.*] The courts of this State shall recognize and enforce an initial or modification decree of a court of another state which had assumed jurisdiction under statutory provisions substantially in accordance with this Act or which was made under factual circumstances meeting the jurisdictional standards of the Act, so long as this decree has not been modified in accordance with jurisdictional standards substantially similar to those of this Act.

### COMMENT

This section and sections 14 and 15 are the key provisions which guarantee a great measure of security and stability of environment to the "interstate child" by discouraging relitigations in other states. See Section 1, and see Ratner, Child Custody in a Federal System, 62 Mich. L. Rev. 795, 828 (1964).

Although the full faith and credit clause may perhaps not require the recognition of out-of-state custody decrees, the states are free to recognize and enforce them. See Restatement of the Law Second, Conflict of Laws, Proposed Official Draft, section 109 (1967), and see the Prefatory Note, *supra*. This section declares as a matter of state law, that custody decrees of sister states will be recognized and enforced. Recognition and enforcement is mandatory if the state in which the prior decree was rendered 1) has adopted this Act, 2) has statutory jurisdictional requirements substantially like this Act, or 3) would have had jurisdiction under the facts of the case if this Act had been the law in the state. Compare Comment, Ford v. Ford: Full Faith and Credit to Child Custody Decrees? 73 Yale LJ. 134, 148 (1963).

"Jurisdiction" or "jurisdictional standards" under this section refers to the requirements of section 3 in the case of initial decrees and to the requirements of sections 3 and 14 in the case of modification decrees. The section leaves open the possibility of discretionary recognition of custody decrees of other states beyond the enumerated situations of mandatory acceptance. For the recognition of custody decrees of other nations, see section 23.

Recognition is accorded to a decree which is valid and binding under section 12. This means, for example, that a court in the state where the father resides will recognize and enforce a custody decree rendered in the home state where the child lives with the mother if the father was duly notified and given enough time to appear in the proceedings. Personal jurisdiction over the father is not required. See comment to section 12. This is in accord with a common interpretation of the inconclusive decision in May v. Anderson, 345 U.S. 528, 73 S. Ct. 840, 97 L. Ed. 1221 (1953). See Restatement of the Law Second, Conflict of Laws, Proposed Official Draft, section 79 and comment thereto, p. 298 (1967). Under this interpretation a state is permitted to recognize a custody decree of another state regardless of lack of personal jurisdiction, as long as due process requirements of notice and opportunity to be heard have been met. See Justice Frankfurter's concurring opinion in May v. Anderson; and compare Clark, Domestic Relations 323-26 (1968), Goodrich, Conflict of Laws 274 (4th ed. by Scoles, 1964); Stumberg, Principles of Conflict of Laws 325 (3rd ed. 1963); and Comment, The Puzzle of Jurisdiction in Child Custody Actions, 38 U. Colo. L. Rev. 541 (1966). The Act emphasizes the need for the personal appearance of the contestants rather than any technical requirement for personal jurisdiction.

The mandate of this section could cause problems if the prior decree is a punitive or disciplinary measure. See Ehrenzweig, Inter-state Recognition of Custody Decrees, 51 Mich. L. Rev. 345, 370 (1953). If, for example, a court grants custody to the mother and after 5 years' of continuous life with the mother the child is awarded to the father by the same court for the sole reason that the mother who had moved to another state upon remarriage had not lived up to the visitation requirements of the decree, courts in other states may be reluctant to recognize the changed decree. See Berlin v. Berlin, 21 N.Y. 2d 371, 235 N.E. 2d 109 (1967); and Stout v. Pate, 120 Cal. App. 2d 699, 261 P. 2d 788 (1953); Compare Moniz v. Moniz, 142 Cal. App. 2d 527, 298 P. 2d 710 (1956). Disciplinary decrees of this type can be avoided under this Act by enforcing the visitation provisions of the decree directly in another state. See Section 15. If the original plan for visitation does not fit the new conditions, a petition for modification of the visiting arrangements would be filed in a court which has jurisdiction, that is, in many cases the original court. See section 14.

SECTION 14. [*Modification of Custody Decree of Another State.*]

**(a) If a court of another state has made a custody decree, a**

court of this State shall not modify that decree unless (1) it appears to the court of this State that the court which rendered the decree does not now have jurisdiction under jurisdictional prerequisites substantially in accordance with this Act or has declined to assume jurisdiction to modify the decree and (2) the court of this State has jurisdiction.

(b) If a court of this State is authorized under subsection (a) and section 8 to modify a custody decree of another state it shall give due consideration to the transcript of the record and other documents of all previous proceedings submitted to it in accordance with section 22.

### Comment

Courts which render a custody decree normally retain continuing jurisdiction to modify the decree under local law. Courts in other states have in the past often assumed jurisdiction to modify the out-of-state decree themselves without regard to the preexisting jurisdiction of the other state. See People ex rel. Halvey v. Halvey, 330 U.S. 610, 67 S. Ct. 903, 91 L. Ed. 1133 (1947). In order to achieve greater stability of custody arrangements and avoid forum shopping, subsection (a) declares that other states will defer to the continuing jurisdiction of the court of another state as long as that state has jurisdiction under the standards of this Act. In other words, all petitions for modification are to be addressed to the prior state if that state has sufficient contact with the case to satisfy section 3. The fact that the court had previously considered the case may be one factor favoring its continued jurisdiction. If, however, all the persons involved have moved away or the contact with the state has otherwise become slight, modification jurisdiction would shift elsewhere. Compare Ratner, Child Custody in a Federal System, 62 Mich. L. Rev. 795, 821-2(1964).

For example, if custody was awarded to the father in state 1 where he continued to live with the children for two years and thereafter his wife kept the children in state 2 for 6-1/2 months (3-1/2 months beyond her visitation privileges) with or without permission of the husband, state 1 has preferred jurisdiction to modify the decree despite the fact that state 2 has in the meantime become the "home state" of the child. If, however, the father also moved away from state 1, that state loses modification jurisdiction interstate, whether or not its jurisdiction continues under local law. See Clark, Domestic Relations 322-23 (1968). Also, if the father in the same case continued to live in state 1, but let his wife keep the children for several years without asserting his custody rights and without visits of the children in state 1, modification jurisdiction of state 1 would cease. Compare Brengle v. Hurst, 408 S. W. 2d 418 (Ky. 1966). The situation would be different if the children had been abducted and their whereabouts could not be discovered by the legal custodian for several years. The abductor would be denied access to the court of another state under section 8(b) and state 1 would have modification jurisdiction in any event under section 3(a) (4). Compare Crocker v. Crocker, 122 Colo. 49, 219 P. 2d 311 (1950).

The prior court has jurisdiction to modify under this section even though its original assumption of jurisdiction did not meet the standards of this Act, as long as it would have jurisdiction *now,* that is, at the time of the petition for modification.

If the state of the prior decree declines to assume jurisdiction to modify the decree, another state with jurisdiction under section 3 can proceed with the case. That is not so if the prior court dismissed the petition on its merits.

Respect for the continuing jurisdiction of another state under this section will serve the purposes of this Act only if the prior court will assume a corresponding obligation to make no changes in the existing custody arrangement which are not required for the good of the child. If the court overturns its own decree in order to discipline a mother or father, with whom the child had lived for years, for failure to comply with an order of the court, the objective of greater stability of custody decrees is not achieved. See Comment to section 13 last paragraph, and cases there cited. See also Sharpe v. Sharpe, 77 Ill. App. 295, 222 N.E. 2d 340 (1966). Under section 15 of this Act an order of a court contained in a custody decree can be directly enforced in another state.

Under subsection (b) transcipts of prior proceedings if received under section 22 are to be considered by the modifying court. The purpose is to give the judge the opportunity to be as fully informed as possible before making a custody decision. "One court will seldom have so much of the story that another's inquiry is unimportant" says Paulsen, Appointment of a Guardian in the Conflict of Laws, 45 Iowa L. Rev. 212, 226 (1960). See also Ehrenzweig, the Interstate Child and Uniform Legislation: A Plea for Extra-Litigious Proceedings, 64 Mich. L. Rev. 1, 6-7 (1965); and Ratner, Legislative Resolution of the Interstate Custody Problem: A Reply to Professor Currie and a Proposed Uniform Act, 38 S. Cal. L. Rev. 183, 202 (1965). How much consideration is "due" this transcript, whether or under what conditions it is received in evidence, are matters of local, internal law which are not affected by this interstate act.

SECTION 15. [*Filing and Enforcement of Custody Decree of Another State.*]

(a) A certified copy of a custody decree of another state may be filed in the office of the clerk of any [District Court, Family Court] of this State. The clerk shall treat the decree in the same manner as a custody decree of the [District Court, Family Court] of this State. A custody decree so filed has the same effect and shall be enforced in like manner as a custody decree rendered by a court of this State.

(b) A person violating a custody decree of another state which makes it necessary to enforce the decree in this State may be required to pay necessary travel and other expenses, including attorneys' fees, incurred by the party entitled to the custody or his witnesses.

## COMMENT

Out-of-state custody decrees which are required to be recognized are enforced by other states. See section 13. Subsection (a) provides a simplified and speedy method of enforcement. It is derived from section 2 of the Uniform Enforcement of Foreign Judgments Act of 1964, 9A U.L.A. 486 (1965). A certified copy of the decree is filed in the appropriate court, and the decree thereupon becomes in effect a decree of the state of filing and is enforceable by any method of enforcement available under the law of that state.

The authority to enforce an out-of-state decree does not include the power to modify it. If modification is desired, the petition must be directed to the court which has jurisdiction to modify under section 14. This does not mean that the state of enforcement may not in an emergency stay enforcement if there is danger of serious mistreatment of the child. See Ratner, Child Custody in a Federal System, 62 Mich. L. Rev. 795, 832-33 (1964).

The right to custody for periods of visitation and other provisions of a custody decree are enforceable in other states in the same manner as the primary right to custody. If visitation privileges provided in the decree have become impractical upon moving to another state, the remedy against automatic enforcement in another state is a petition in the proper court to modify visitation arrangements to fit the new conditions.

Subsection (b) makes it clear that the financial burden of enforcement of a custody decree may be shifted to the wrongdoer. Compare 2 Armstrong, California Family Law 328 (1966 Suppl.), and *Crocker v. Crocker,* 195 F. 2d 236 (1952).

SECTION 16. [*Registry of Out-of-State Custody Decrees and Proceedings.*] The clerk of each [District Court, Family Court] shall maintain a registry in which he shall enter the following:

(1) certified copies of custody decrees of other states received for filing;

(2) communications as to the pendency of custody proceedings in other states;

(3) communications concerning a finding of inconvenient forum by a court of another state; and

(4) other communications or documents concerning custody proceedings in another state which may affect the jurisdiction of a court of this State or the disposition to be made by it in a custody proceeding.

COMMENT

The purpose of this section is to gather all information concerning out-of-state custody cases which reaches a court in one designated place. The term "registry" is derived from section 35 of the Uniform Reciprocal Enforcement of Support Act of 1958, 9C U.L.A. 61 (1967 Suppl.) Another term may be used if desired without affecting the uniformity of the Act. The information in the registry is usually incomplete since it contains only those documents which have been specifically requested or which have otherwise found their way to the state. It is therefore necessary in most cases for the court to seek additional information elsewhere.

SECTION 17. [*Certified Copies of Custody Decree.*] The Clerk of the [District Court, Family Court] of this State, at the request of the court of another state or at the request of any person who is affected by or has a legitimate interest in a custody decree, shall certify and forward a copy of the decree to that court or person.

SECTION 18. [*Taking Testimony in Another State.*] In addition to other procedural devices available to a party, any party to the proceeding or a guardian ad litem or other representative of the child may adduce testimony of witnesses, including parties and the child, by deposition or otherwise, in another state. The court on its own motion may direct that the testimony of a person be taken in another state and may prescribe the manner in which and the terms upon which the testimony shall be taken.

### Comment

Sections 18 to 22 are derived from sections 3.01 and 3.02 of the Uniform Interstate and International Procedure Act, 9B U.L.A. 305, 321, 326 (1966); from ideas underlying the Uniform Reciprocal Enforcement of Support Act; and from Ehrenzweig, the Interstate Child and Uniform Legislation: A Plea for Extralitigious Proceedings, 64 Mich. L. Rev. 1 (1965). They are designed to fill the partial vacuum which inevitably exists in cases involving an "interstate child" since part of the essential information about the child and his relationship to other persons is always in another state. Even though jurisdiction is assumed under sections 3 and 7 in the state where much (or most) of the pertinent facts are readily available, some important evidence will unavoidably be elsewhere.

Section 18 is derived from portions of section 3.01 of the Uniform Interstate and International Procedure Act, 9B U.L.A. 305, 321. The first sentence relates to depositions, written interrogatories and other discovery devices which may be used by parties or representatives of the child. The procedural rules of the state where the device is used are applicable under this sentence. The second sentence empowers the court itself to initiate the gathering of out-of-state evidence which is often not supplied by the parties in order to give the court a complete picture of the child's situation, especially as it relates to a custody claimant who lives in another state.

Section 19. [*Hearings and Studies in Another State; Orders to Appear.*]

(a) A court of this State may request the appropriate court of another state to hold a hearing to adduce evidence, to order a party to produce or give evidence under other procedures of that state, or to have social studies made with respect to the custody of a child involved in proceedings pending in the court of this State; and to forward to the court of this State certified copies of the transcript of the record of the hearing, the evidence otherwise adduced, or any social studies prepared in compliance with the request. The cost of the services may be assessed against the parties or, if necessary, ordered paid by the [County, State].

(b) A court of this State may request the appropriate court of another state to order a party to custody proceedings pending in the court of this State to appear in the proceedings, and if that party has physical custody of the child, to appear with the child. The request may state that travel and other necessary expenses of the party and of the child whose appearance is desired will be assessed against another party or will otherwise be paid.

**Comment**

Section 19 relates to assistance sought by a court of the forum state from a court of another state. See comment to section 18. Subsection (a) covers any kind of evidentiary procedure available under the law of the assisting state which may aid the court in the requesting state, including custody investigations (social studies) if authorized by the law of the other state. Under what conditions reports of social studies and other evidence collected under this subsection are admissible in the requesting state, is a matter of internal state law not covered in this interstate statute. Subsection (b) serves to bring parties and the child before the requesting court, backed up by the assisting court's contempt powers. See section 11.

Section 20 [*Assistance to Courts of Other States.*]

(a) Upon request of the court of another state the courts of this State which are competent to hear custody matters may order a person in this State to appear at a hearing to adduce evidence or to produce or give evidence under other procedures availiable in this State [or may order social studies to be made for use in a custody proceeding in another state]. A certified copy of the transcript of the record of the hearing or the evidence otherwise adduced [and any social studies prepared] shall be forwarded by the clerk of the court to the requesting court.

(b) A person within this State may voluntarily give his testimony or statement in this State for use in a custody proceeding outside this state.

(c) Upon request of the court of another state a competent court of this State may order a person in this State to appear alone or with the child in a custody proceeding in another state. The court may condition compliance with the request upon assurance by the other state that state travel and other necessary expenses will be advanced or reimbursed.

**Comment**

Section 20 is the counterpart of section 19. It empowers local courts to give help to out-of-state courts in custody cases. See comments to sections 18 and 19. The references to social studies have been placed in brackets so that states without authorization to make social studies outside of juvenile court proceedings may omit them if they wish. Subsection (b) reaffirms the existing freedom of persons within the United States to give evidence for use in proceedings elsewhere. It is derived from section 3.02 (b) of the Interstate and International Procedure Act, 9B U.L.A. 327 (1966).

Section 21. [*Preservation of Documents for Use in Other States.*] In any custody proceeding in this State the court shall preserve the pleadings, orders and decrees, any record that has been made of its hearings, social studies, and other pertinent documents

**until the child reaches [18, 21] years of age. Upon appropriate request of the court of another state the court shall forward to the other court certified copies of any or all of such documents.**

COMMENT

See comments to sections 18 and 19. Documents are to be preserved until the child is old enough that further custody disputes are unlikely. A lower figure than the ones suggested in the brackets may be inserted.

SECTION 22. [*Request for Court Records of Another State.*] If a custody decree has been rendered in another state concerning a child involved in a custody proceeding pending in a court of this State, the court of this State upon taking jurisdiction of the case shall request of the court of the other state a certified copy of the transcript of any court record and other documents mentioned in section 21.

COMMENT

This is the counterpart of section 21. See comments to sections 18, 19, and 14(b).

SECTION 23. [*International Application.*] The general policies of this Act extend to the international area. The provisions of this Act relating to the recognition and enforcement of custody decrees of other states apply to custody decrees and decrees inolving legal institutions similar in nature to custody institutions rendered by appropriate authorities of other nations if reasonable notice and opportunity to be heard were given to all affected persons.

COMMENT

Not all the provisions of the Act lend themselves to direct application in international custody disputes; but the basic policies of avoiding jurisdictional conflict and multiple litigation are as strong if not stronger when children are moved back and forth from one country to another by feuding relatives. Compare Application of Lang, 9 App. Div. 2d 401, 193 N.Y.S. 2d 763 (1959) and Swindle v. Bradley, 240 Ark. 903, 403 S.W. 2d 63 (1966).

The first sentence makes the general policies of the Act applicable to international cases. This means that the substance of section 1 and the principles underlying provisions like sections 6, 7, 8, and 14(a), are to be followed when some of the persons involved are in a foreign country or a foreign custody proceeding is pending.

The second sentence declares that custody decrees rendered in other nations by appropriate authorities (which may be judicial or administrative tribunals) are recognized and enforced in this country. The only prerequisite is that reasonable notice and opportunity to be heard was given to the persons affected. It is also to be understood that the foreign tribunal had jurisdiction under its own law rather than under section 3 of this Act. Compare Restatement of the Law Second, Conflict of Laws, Proposed Official Draft, sections 10, 92, 98, and 109(2) (1967). Compare also Goodrich, Conflict of Laws 390-93 (4th ed., Scoles, 1964).

[SECTION 24. [*Priority.*] Upon the request of a party to a custody proceeding which raises a question of existence or exercise of jurisdiction under this Act the case shall be given calendar priority and handled expeditiously.]

COMMENT

Judicial time spent in determining which court has or should exercise jurisdiction often prolongs the period of uncertainty and turmoil in a child's life more than is necessary. The need for speedy adjudication exists, of course, with respect to all aspects of child custody litigation. The priority requirement is limited to jurisdictional questions because an all encompassing priority would be beyond the scope of this Act. Since some states may have or wish to adopt a statutory provision or court rule of wider scope, this section is placed in brackets and may be omitted.

SECTION 25. [*Severability.*] If any provision of this Act or the application thereof to any person or circumstance is held invalid, its invalidity does not affect other provisions or applications of the Act which can be given effect without the invalid provision or application, and to this end the provisions of this Act are severable.

SECTION 26. [*Short Title.*] This Act may be cited as the Uniform Child Custody Jurisdiction Act.

SECTION 27. [*Repeal.*] The following acts and parts of acts are repealed:

(1)

(2)

(3)

SECTION 28. [*Time of Taking Effect.*] This Act shall take effect. . . .

## TABLE OF STATE CODE CITATIONS AND VARIATIONS (EXCLUDING MINOR, CONFORMING VARIATIONS)

Note: Unless otherwise labeled, section numbers refer to sections of the standard Uniform Act as drafted by the Commissioners.

### ALABAMA:

Public Act 92(HB 154(1980)), 34 Ala. Code §30-20-2 et seq.
§5 requires 20 days' notice. §20 omits the bracketed phrases concerning social-worker studies. Omits §24 on court calendar priority.

### ALASKA:

A.S. §§25.30.010–25.30.910 (1977).
Omits subsec. 1(b) guiding construction. Omits Subsec. 3(a)(2) creating "significant connection" jurisdiction, and ties 3(a)(3) "emergency" to Alaska code "child in need of aid" provisions. Adds consideration of ascertainable language and education differences to §4 "reasonable opportunity to be heard" provision. Rewrites §5 to conform to local law of notice. Rewrites §8(a) to make pre-decree removal the same as Subsec. 8(b) post-decree removal, and require jurisdiction for an initial decree be declined except in emergency as defined by Alaska child abuse/neglect laws. Removes "best interest" exception from 8(b) "unclean hands" bar to modification decree. Adds provision to §9 requiring all such information be made available to both parties' counsel. Removes §13 exception for modified decrees. Adds clerk's fee provision to §17. Conditions §20 sending of court record upon receipt of payment. Reimbursement provisions added to §§21 and 22, §24 conditions docketing priority on conformity to Alaska court rules. §5 requires 20 days' notice.

### ARIZONA:

ARS 8-401–8-424 (1978).
§3 references to home state speak of "domicile or home state." §5 requires 20 days' notice. Omits bracketed language of §20(a) on preparation of social studies. Omits §24.

## ARKANSAS:

STAT. ANN. §§34-2701–2725 (1979 Supp.)(1979).

## CALIFORNIA:

West's Ann. Civil Code §§5150–5174 (1973).
§5 provides 10 days' notice. Adds to §8 two lengthy Subsections providing: (1) that when a petitioner for initial decree is turned down, the other parent and prosecutor in the home state shall be notified and the petitioner can be required to attend proceedings there, but that if no home-state request for such attendance is received within a reasonable time, California court can entertain the petition; (2) that when the petition is for a modification decree, the court shall similarly notify custodial parent and prosecutor, and require home state appearance, and can place child in foster home for "a few days" pending return.
§11 backs up order-to-appear provisions with arrest-warrant power.
§20 omits bracketed language, and §20(c) adds an arrest-warrant power.

## COLORADO:

CRS 1973, §§14-13-101–126 (1973).
§5 provides 20 days' notice.

## CONNECTICUT:

CGSA §§46(b)-90–114 (1978).
§5 provides 12 days' notice.

## DELAWARE:

13 Delaware Code §§1901–1925 (1976).
§1(a)(3) adds at end "which have enacted the UCCJA." §5 provides 20 days' notice.

## FLORIDA:

FSA §§61.1302–.1348 (West Supp. 1978)(1977).
§1 omits Subsection(b). §3(a)(3) omits bracketed language. §5(b) provides 20 days' notice. §24 on priority omitted.

## GEORGIA:

Ga. CODE ANN. §§74-501–525 (1979).
§5(b) provides 30 days' notice. §16(1) and §22 require exemplified, rather than certified copies.

## HAWAII:

Rev. Stat. §§ 583-1-26 (Supp. 1975)(1973).
§1(b) provides the Act's principles shall apply only between states having similar legislation. §5(b) provides 20 days' notice. §9 omits "under oath" requirement.

## IDAHO:

CODE §§5-1001-1025 (1979)(1977).
§5(b) provides 20 days' notice. §20 omits bracketed language.

## ILLINOIS:

HB 684 (public act 81-541)(1979).
Though Illinois originally had a non-conforming version of the Act, embodying the pertinent provisions of the Uniform Marriage and Divorce Act (§401 of the standard UMDA—see FLR RF 201: 0001 or BNA *Desk Guide to the Uniform Marriage and Divorce Act* (1974), p. 41), the standard Act has since been adopted in its place. §5 provides for 10 days' notice.

## INDIANA:

IND. CODE ANN. §§31-1-11.6-1-24 (Burns Supp. 1979)(1977).
§5(a)(4) omits bracketed language; §5(b) provides 20 days' notice.

## IOWA:

CODE ANN. §§598A.1-.25 (West Supp. 1979)(1977).
Rewrites §5 on notice to tie into Iowa law, requires 20 days' notice.

## KANSAS:

STAT. §§38-1301-1326 (Supp. 1979)(1979).
§5 requires 30 days' notice. Sections are added to keep a court from exercising jurisdiction in parental rights termination cases except in acccordance with §3 criteria, and requiring that any petition or answer filed in a divorce case wherein the parties have children shall contain the UCCJA §9 affidavit information. The state's general parens patriae "care of children" statute is also amended to limit exercise of jurisdiction to those appropriate under the UCCJA. Similarly, the state's statute on decrees in a "divisible divorce" is amended to conform to the UCCJA concept of jurisdiction.

## KENTUCKY:

Senate Bill 42(1980), adding sections to K.R.S. Ch. 403.
It omits §24 on calendar priority. §5 gives 20 days' notice. Earlier, the

Kentucky Act had included several provisions inconsistent with the official version of the UCCJA, but these have since been repealed.

### LOUISIANA:

RSA §§13:1700-:1724 (West. Supp. 1979)(1978).
§5 requires 10 days' notice. §15 provides discretionary authority for temporary custody in the welfare department when a foreign decree is filed for enforcement and there is probable cause to believe the parent may flee Louisiana.

### MAINE:

19 RSA, §§801-825 (Supp. 1979)(1979).
§5 provides 20 days' notice.

### MARYLAND:

ANN. CODE art. 16 §§184-207 (Supp. 1979)(1975).
Omits §5 on notice. §6(a) includes an emergency and abandonment exception.

### MICHIGAN:

COMP. LAWS ANN. §§600.651-.673 (Supp. 1979)(1976).
§5(b) provides 20 days' notice. §6(a) includes an emergency exception. Omits §24 on priority.

### MINNESOTA:

STAT. ANN. §§518A.01-.25 (West Supp. 1979)(1977).
§5(b) provides 20 days' notice. §9(a) is worded differently to allow avoidance of the affidavit procedure if a moving party alleges a good faith belief that there is no jurisdictional question.

### MISSOURI:

ANN. STAT. §§452-440-550 (Vernon Supp. 1979)(1978).
Omits §1 statement of purpose and principles governing construction. §5 simply allows the existing Missouri personal and postal modes of service. §23 concerning international application is omitted.

### MONTANA:

CODE ANN. §§40-7-101-125 (1979)(1977).
§2 excludes parental rights termination/adoption proceedings from the definition of "custody proceeding." §5(b) provides 10 days' notice.

## NEBRASKA:

REV. STAT. §§43-1201–1225 (Supp. 1979)(1979).
§5 notice provisions incorporate applicable Nebraska statutes on service of process, adding a provision for service by mail.

## NEVADA:

1979 STATS. ch. 85 (Amends Title 11 NRS)(1979).
§5 provides 20 days' notice. §23 substitutes "other nations" for the enigmatic phrase "international area." Additional sections at the end provide for injunctive relief when it is probable that a custody decree might be defied or otherwise frustrated, provide a strong pro-female tender years presumption, authorize bond to secure performance ordered under the Act, make the "best interest" custody criterion statutory, and authorize custody decree modification at all times.

## NEW HAMPSHIRE:

H.B. 743; (RSA Ch. 458-A)(1979).
Notice section provides 20 days' notice and service by mail, and incorporates applicable New Hampshire notice statutes.

## NEW JERSEY:

STAT. ANN. §§2A: 34-28–52 (West 1979)(1979).
Omits §1(a)(9) and 1(b). §3 omits bracketed material. §4 requires notice under the provisions of New Jersey court rules. §5 omits language concerning requirement of a receipt. §5(a)(3) and (4) omit bracketed language. §5(b) requires 20 days' notice, or less if court deems situation emergent. §19 adds provision that appearance in another state does not mean waiver of jurisdictional objections. §24 is omitted.

## NEW MEXICO:

SB 83 (1981).
Minor variations in §§5, 8, 9. Omits §19. Applies only between UCCJA states.

## NEW YORK:

DOM. REL. LAW §§75a-z (McKinney Supp. 1979)(1977).
§2 excludes parental rights termination/adoption/dependency/neglect proceedings from definition of "custodial proceedings." §4 adds provision that anyone given notice and an opportunity to be heard shall be deemed a party. §5 is rewritten to incorporate New York ser-

vice rules. §9 allows its requirements to be dispensed with in a divorce case where custody is not contested.

## NORTH CAROLINA:

GEN. STAT. §§50A-1-25 (Supp. 1979)(1979).
Adds a section saying that the court has power to issue immediate or interlocutory custody orders. §4 omits final sentence. §5 on notice provides for notice under applicable North Carolina law. §11(a) and 12 are not restricted to in-state parties. §24 is omitted.

## NORTH DAKOTA:

CENT. CODE §§14-14-1-26 (Repl. Vol. 1971)(1969).
An additional section makes removal of child a class C felony. §5(b) provides 20 days' notice.

## OHIO:

REV. CODE ANN. §§3109.21-.37 (Baldwin Supp. 1978)(1977).
Omits §1 on purpose and interpretation. §5 on notice incorporates Ohio rules, provides 20 days. §8(a) omits the word "reprehensible." §23 on international application omitted.

## OKLAHOMA:

10 O.S. §§1601-1627 (1980).
A section added between §§ 1 and 2 provides that the Act applies to all custody proceedings brought within Oklahoma, and makes the Act applicable intrastate to inter-county disputes. An addition to §3 (10 O.S. §1605D) makes best interest of the child the custody criterion. 10 days' notice is provided for. §24 on priority is omitted. A criminal provision making the violation of a custody order with intent to deprive the lawful custodian of custody a felony is added.

## OREGON:

REV. STAT. §§109.700-.930 (Supp. 1977)(1973).
§5 provides 20 days' notice.

## PENNSYLVANIA:

11 STAT. ANN, §§2301-2325 (Purdon Supp. 1979)(1977).
§5(b) provides 10 days' notice. §8(a) omits "reprehensible conduct" and substitutes "conduct intended to benefit his position in a custody hearing." §8(b) includes an exception in the last sentence for a show-

ing by the petitioner that "conditions in the custodial household are physically or emotionally harmful."

## RHODE ISLAND:

GEN. LAWS §§15-14-1–26 (Supp. 1978)(1978).
§5(b) provides 20 days' notice. Special wording in §13.

## SOUTH DAKOTA:

COMPILED LAWS ANN. §§26-5-5–52 (Supp. 1979)(1978).
§5(a)(4) omits bracketed language. §5(b) omits first bracketed passage, and gives 20 days' notice. §5(d) and §23 omitted.

## TENNESSEE:

HB 643 (1979 public acts ch. 383(pp. 945-962))(1979).
§3 specifically declares home state priority over "significant connection" jurisdiction. §3 also expressly declares that jurisdiction shall not be exercised to modify a foreign decree except in accordance with the non-modification article (§14 of the standard text and §15 of the Tennessee version). A section has been added as number 4, which limits the jurisdiction of courts to suspend temporarily the enforcement of an existing decree and make a temporary decree to 60 days—and then only if a child physically present in the state has been abandoned or needs emergency protection from serious harm to life or limb. This section also expressly decrees that to get a permanent decree, a party must file in whatever state has jurisdiction under the §3 criteria. §5 (§6 of the Tennessee act) provides 20 days' notice.

## UTAH:

HB 51 (1980).
§5 gives 10 days' notice.

## VERMONT:

15 VSA §§1031–1053 (1979).
§5 requires 20 days' notice.

## VIRGINIA:

CODE ANN. §§20-125–146 (Cum. Supp. 1979)(1979).
Omits §1 and §24. §2 substitutes "decrees" for "instructions." §5 omits service by mail and requires 21 days' notice. §7(c) omits (5). Subsection 7(i) omits reference to custody registry.

## WASHINGTON:

1979 WASH. LAWS ch. 98 (1979).
§5 requires 10 days' notice. Omits §24 on calendar priority. §8 adds provisions for ordering physical return of the child. §11 adds language providing for arrest and compelled appearance, as does §20.

## WEST VIRGINIA:

HB 785 (1981).

## WISCONSIN:

WISC. STAT. ANN. §§822.01–.25 (West Supp. 1979)(1976).
§1(a)(3) specifically declares the "maximum contacts" theory, observing that one purpose of the statute is to "assure . . . that courts of this state decline the exercise of jurisdiction when a child and family have a closer connection with another state." §5 requires 10 days' notice.

## WYOMING:

WYO. STAT. §§20-5-101–125 (Repl. Vol. 1977)(1973).
§5 requires 20 days' notice.

## RELATED STATUTORY SCHEMES

### FEDERAL LEGISLATION: THE WALLOP AMENDMENT

Against a background of near-total state adoption of the Uniform Child Custody Jurisdiction Act and pending U.S. Supreme Court review of the question whether the Constitution requires state courts to give foreign custody orders full faith and credit, there is now a federal statute requiring both. The so-called Wallop Bill, which in some form or another had been considered and rejected by Congress in every session for many years, finally passed as a rider to the Pneumococcol Vaccine Medicare Coverage Act, HR. 8406, and was signed by the President on December 29, 1980.

The anti-forum-shopping provision of this bill is definitely an odd piece of federal legislation. It amends Title 28 U.S.C., the Judicial Code, to require by federal statute that state courts give full faith and credit to the custody decrees of other states. It then goes on to explain what this requirement shall mean by incorporating several key sections of the UCCJA, such as §2 on definitions, §3 on jurisdiction, and §§12 through 14 on res judicata, recognition and nonmodification. The provision of Section 6 forbidding simultaneous proceedings on custody in two or more states is also incorporated.

Other parts of the bill require the Federal Parent Locator Service to be made available for locating parents who flee with their children, and declare it to be congressional intent that the FBI track down such parents as violators of the criminal code section on interstate flight to avoid prosecution, 18 USC §1073. The comity requirement will add a §1738A to 28 U.S.C. and the parent locator provision will amend Title IV-D of the Social Security Act by adding a §463.

### PARENTAL KIDNAPING PREVENTION ACT OF 1980<br>PL 96-611

#### FINDINGS AND PURPOSES

Sec. 7.(a) The Congress finds that—

(1) there is a large and growing number of cases annually involving disputes between persons claiming rights of custody and

visitation of children under the laws, and in the courts, of different States, the District of Columbia, the Commonwealth of Puerto Rico, and the territories and possessions of the United States;

(2) the laws and practices by which the courts of those jurisdictions determine their jurisdiction to decide such disputes, and the effect to be given the decisions of such disputes by the courts of other jurisdictions, are often inconsistent and conflicting;

(3) those characteristics of the law and practice in such cases, along with the limits imposed by a Federal system on the authority of each such jurisdiction to conduct investigations and take other actions outside its own boundaries, contribute to a tendency of parties involved in such disputes to frequently resort to the seizure, restraint, concealment, and interstate transportation of children, the disregard of court orders, excessive relitigation of cases, obtaining of conflicting orders by the courts of various jurisdictions, and interstate travel and communication that is so expensive and time consuming as to disrupt their occupations and commercial activities; and

(4) among the results of those conditions and activities are the failure of the courts of such jurisdictions to give full faith and credit to the judicial proceedings of the other jurisdictions, the deprivation of rights of liberty and property without due process of law, burdens on commerce among such jurisdictions and with foreign nations, and harm to the welfare of children and their parents and other custodians.

(b) For those reasons it is necessary to establish a national system for locating parents and children who travel from one such jurisdiction to another and are concealed in connection with such disputes, and to establish national standards under which the courts of such jurisdictions will determine their jurisdiction to decide such disputes and the effect to be given by each such jurisdiction to such decisions by the courts of other such jurisdictions.

(c) The general purposes of sections 6 to 10 of this Act are to—

(1) promote cooperation between State courts to the end that a determination of custody and visitation is rendered in the State which can best decide the case in the interest of the child;

(2) promote and expand the exchange of information and other forms of mutual assistance between States which are concerned with the same child;

(3) facilitate the enforcement of custody and visitation decrees of sister States;

(4) discourage continuing interstate controversies over child custody in the interest of greater stability of home environment and of secure family relationships for the child;

(5) avoid jurisdictional competition and conflict between State courts in matters of child custody and visitation which have in the past resulted in the shifting of children from State to State with harmful effects on their well-being; and

(6) deter interstate abductions and other unilateral removals of children undertaken to obtain custody and visitation awards.

FULL FAITH AND CREDIT GIVEN TO CHILD CUSTODY DETERMINATIONS

SEC. 8. (a) Chapter 115 of title 28, United States Code, is amended by adding immediately after section 1738 the following new section:

**"§1738A. Full faith and credit given to child custody determination**

"(a) The appropriate authorities of every State shall enforce according to its terms, and shall not modify except as provided in subsection (f) of this section, any child custody determination made consistently with the provisions of this section by a court of another State.

"(b) As used in this section, the term—

"(1) 'child' means a person under the age of eighteen;

"(2) 'contestant' means a person, including a parent, who claims a right to custody or visitation of a child;

"(3) 'custody determination' means a judgment, decree, or other order of a court providing for the custody or visitation of a child, and includes permanent and temporary orders, and initial orders and modifications;

"(4) 'home State' means the State in which, immediately preceding the time involved, the child lived with his parents, a parent, or a person acting as parent, for at least six consecutive months, and in the case of a child less than six months old, the State in which the child lived from birth with any of such persons. Periods of temporary absence of any of such persons are counted as part of the six-month or other period;

"(5) 'modification' and 'modify' refer to a custody determination which modifies, replaces, supersedes, or otherwise is made subsequent to, a prior custody determination concerning the same child, whether made by the same court or not;

"(6) 'person acting as a parent' means a person, other than a parent, who has physical custody of a child and who has either been awarded custody by a court or claims a right to custody;

"(7) 'physical custody' means actual possession and control of a child; and

"(8) 'State' means a State of the United States, the District of Columbia, the Commonwealth of Puerto Rico, or a territory or possession of the United States.

"(c) A child custody determination made by a court of a State is consistent with the provisions of this section only if—

"(1) such court has jurisdiction under the law of such State; and

"(2) one of the following conditions is met:

"(A) such State (i) is the home State of the child on the date of the commencement of the proceeding, or (ii) had been the child's home State within six months before the date of the commencement of the proceeding and the child is absent from such State because of his removal or retention by a contestant or for other reasons, and a contestant continues to live in such State;

"(B)(i) it appears that no other State would have jurisdiction under subparagraph (A), and (ii) it is in the best interest of the child that a court of such State assume jurisdiction because (I) the child and his parents, or the child and at least one contestant, have a significant connection with such State other than mere physical presence in such State, and (II) there is available in such State substantial evidence concerning the child's present or future care, protection, training, and personal relationships;

"(C) the child is physically present in such State and (i) the child has been abandoned, or (ii) it is necessary in an emergency to protect the child because he has been subjected to or threatened with mistreatment or abuse;

"(D)(i) it appears that no other State would have jurisdiction under subparagraph (A), (B), (C), or (E), or another State has declined to exercise jurisdiction on the ground that the State whose jurisdiction is in issue is the more appropriate forum to determine the custody of the child, and (ii) it is in the best interest of the child that such court assume jurisdiction; or

"(E) the court has continuing jurisdiction prusuant to subsection (d) of this section.

"(d) The jurisdiction of a court of a State which has made a child custody determination consistently with the provisions of this section continues as long as the requirement of subsection (c)(1) of this section continues to be met and such State remains the residence of the child or of any contestant.

"(e) Before a child custody determination is made, reasonable notice and opportunity to be heard shall be given to the contestants, any parent whose parental rights have not been previously terminated and any person who has physical custody of a child.

"(f) A court of a State may modify a determination of the custody of the same child made by a court of another State, if—

"(1) it has jurisdiction to make such a child custody determination; and

"(2) the court of the other State no longer has jurisdiction, or it has declined to exercise such jurisdiction to modify such determination.

"(g) A court of a State shall not exercise jurisdiction in any proceeding for a custody determination commenced during the pendency of a proceeding in a court of another State where such court of that other State is exercising jurisdiction consistently with the provisions of this section to make a custody determination.".

(b) The table of sections at the beginning of chapter 115 of title 28, United States Code, is amended by inserting after the item relating to section 1738 the following new item:

"1738A. Full faith and credit given to child custody determinations.".

(c) In furtherance of the purposes of section 1738A of title 28, United States Code, as added by subsection (a) of this section, State courts are encouraged to—

(1) afford priority to proceedings for custody determinations; and

(2) award to the person entitled to custody or visitation pursuant to a custody determination which is consistent with the provisions of such section 1738A, necessary travel expenses, attorneys' fees, costs of private investigations, witness fees or expenses, and other expenses incurred in connection with such custody determination in any case in which—

(A) a contestant has, without the consent of the person entitled to custody or visitation pursuant to a custody determination which is consistent with the provisions of such section 1738A, (i) wrongfully removed the child from the physical custody of such person, or (ii) wrongfully retained the child after a visit or other temporary relinquishment of physical custody; or

(B) the court determines it is appropriate.

USE OF FEDERAL PARENT LOCATOR SERVICE IN CONNECTION WITH THE ENFORCEMENT OR DETERMINATION OF CHILD CUSTODY AND IN CASES OF PARENTAL KIDNAPING OF A CHILD

SEC. 9. (a) Section 454 of the Social Security Act is amended—

(1) by striking out "and" at the end of paragraph (15);

(2) by striking out the period at the end of paragraph (16) and inserting in lieu thereof "; and"; and

(3) by inserting after paragraph (16) the following new paragraph:

"(17) in the case of a State which has in effect an agreement with the Secretary entered into pursuant to section 463 for the use of the Parent Locator Service established under section 453, to accept and transmit to the Secretary requests for information authorized under the provisions of the agreement to be furnished by such Service to authorized persons, and to impose and collect (in accordance with regulations of the Secretary) a fee sufficient to cover the costs to the State and to the Secretary incurred by reason of such requests, to transmit to the Secretary from time to time (in accordance with such regulations) so much of the fees collected as are attributable to such costs to the Secretary so incurred, and during the period that such agreement is in effect, otherwise to comply with such agreement and regulations of the Secretary with respect thereto.".

(b) Part D of title IV of the Social Security Act is amended by adding at the end thereof the following new section:

"USE OF FEDERAL PARENT LOCATOR SERVICE IN CONNECTION WITH THE ENFORCEMENT OR DETERMINATION OF CHILD CUSTODY AND IN CASES OF PARENTAL KIDNAPING OF A CHILD

"SEC. 463. (a) The Secretary shall enter into an agreement with any State which is able and willing to do so, under which the services of the Parent Locator Service established under section 453 shall be made available to such State for the purpose of determining the whereabouts of any absent parent or child when such information is to be used to locate such parent or child for the purpose of—

"(1) enforcing any State or Federal law with respect to the unlawful taking or restraint of a child; or

"(2) making or enforcing a child custody determination.

"(b) An agreement entered into under this section shall provide that the State agency described in section 454 will, under procedures prescribed by the Secretary in regulations, receive and transmit to the Secretary requests from authorized persons for information as to (or useful in determining) the whereabouts of any absent parent or child when such information is to be used to locate such parent or child for the purpose of—

"(1) enforcing any State or Federal law with respect to the unlawful taking or restraint of a child; or

"(2) making or enforcing a child custody determination.

"(c) Information authorized to be provided by the Secretary under this section shall be subject to the same conditions with respect to disclosure as information authorized to be provided under section 453, and a request for information by the Secretary under this section shall be considered to be a request for information under section 453 which is authorized to be provided under such section. Only information as to the most recent address and place of employment of any absent parent or child shall be provided under this section.

"(d) For purposes of this section—

"(1) the term 'custody determination' means a judgment, decree, or other order of a court providing for the custody or visitation of the child, and includes permanent and temporary orders, and initial orders and modification;

"(2) the term 'authorized person' means—

"(A) any agent or attorney of any State having an agreement under this section, who has the duty or authority under the law of such State to enforce a child custody determination;

"(B) any court having jurisdiction to make or enforce such a child custody determination, or any agent of such court; and

"(C) any agent or attorney of the United States, or of a State having an agreement under this section, who has the duty or authority to investigate, enforce, or bring a prosecution with respect to the unlawful taking or restraint of a child.".

(c) Section 455(a) of such Act is amended by adding after paragraph (3) the following: "except that no amount shall be paid to any State on account of amounts expended to carry out an agreement which it has entered into pursuant to section 463.".

(d) No agreement entered into under section 463 of the Social

Security Act shall become effective before the date on which section 1738A of title 28, United States Code (as added by this title) becomes effective.

### PARENTAL KIDNAPING

SEC. 10.(a) In view of the findings of the Congress and the purposes of sections 6 to 10 of this Act set forth in section 302, the Congress hereby expressly declares its intent that section 1073 of title 18, United States Code, apply to cases involving parental kidnaping and interstate or international flight to avoid prosecution under applicable State felony statutes.

(b) The Attorney General of the United States, not later than 120 days after the date of the enactment of this section (and once every 6 months during the 3-year period following such 120-day period), shall submit a report to the Congress with respect to steps taken to comply with the intent of the Congress set forth in subsection (a). Each such report shall include—

(1) data relating to the number of applications for complaints under section 1073 of title 18, United States Code, in cases involving parental kidnaping;

(2) data relating to the number of complaints issued in such cases; and

(3) such other information as may assist in describing the activities of the Department of Justice in conformance with such intent.

### TECHNICAL AMENDMENTS AND AMENDMENTS RELATING TO CHILD SUPPORT AUDITS

(Omitted)

## COMMENTARY

The Wallop Amendment, attempting to affect state courts in a way that federal legislation has never done before, will doubtless be subject to constitutional challenge (unless the U.S. Supreme Court in the Webb case clarifies this entire subject in a useful way). The defense of its intended operation will of course be on the basis of the U.S. Constitution's Article VI law of the land clause, which makes federal statutes as well as constitutional provisions capable of overriding inconsistent state law. Of course Article VI is not capable of supporting independently, by a circularity of reasoning, a federal power that does not constitutionally exist, and the ensuing debate would perhaps be between those asserting a Tenth Amendment limitation and those asserting an Article I section 8 general welfare/interstate commerce implied power.

One interesting respect in which the Uniform Act and the federal statute differ might possibly provide a point of friction between the two. While it could be argued that the UCCJA leaves home state and "significant connection" jurisdiction of equal force and value (for the counter-argument, see the discussion at page [00], above), the federal statute, by a very slight difference of wording, makes express and exclusive the priority of home state jurisdiction over the other jurisdictions. This mandatory priority is created by the first twelve words—i.e., clause (i)—of 28 U.S.C. § 1738A(c)(2)(B), which reads "it appears that no other State would have jurisdiction under subparagraph (A) and."

The various court opinions discussed above which have found and exercised significant-connection jurisdiction despite there being a home state elsewhere would find their interpretation of the Uniform Act thus in conflict with PL 97-611 on this point.

## ADDITIONAL RESOURCE

Those interested in obtaining advice on how to proceed to take full advantage of the Uniform Act and the federal statute are not without resources. The National Legal Resource Center for Child Advocacy and Protection, an American Bar Association-sponsored project at 1800 M Street, Washington, D.C. 20036, has begun a federally-funded Child Custody Project which intends not only to serve an important public education function in the area of UCCJA/Wallop Amendment technique, but also to serve as a clearing house for information on interstate custody law and litigation methods. The project's telephone number is (202) 331-2250.

# INTERNATIONAL CONVENTIONS

## (MULTILATERAL CHILD ABDUCTION TREATIES)

### *THE HAGUE CONVENTION*

Late in 1980, negotiations in Europe produced the final text of an international convention to remedy child-snatching. The United States was able to secure some of the changes its delegation had argued for in the text of the treaty. The Convention on the Civil Aspects of International Child Abduction is a treaty which State Department officials have been authorized to sign for the United States, but it would then have to be ratified by the U.S. Senate. It operates more immediately and directly than the Uniform Child Custody Jurisdiction Act, which primarily discourages child-snatching by making subsequent legitimation of the act very difficult. The convention instead requires countries simply to return children who have been taken by one parent from the country of their habitual residence.

The treaty will have an initial life of only five years, and the U.S. Senate ratification could take as long as two years, so that the U.S. should have a trial period of approximately three years to see whether the provisions of the convention are ones it could live with. Right now only Switzerland, Greece, France, and Canada have signed the convention. The convention will go into operation once three countries have not only signed but ratified it.

Implementation of the treaty in the United States apparently will require some federal legislation, since the question of whether federal or state courts should be the ones to make determinations under the treaty is now very much open. Statutorily, a "right arising under a treaty" is within the "federal question" jurisdiction of U.S. district courts. Yet clearly it has always been state courts that have made custody determinations in the United States, and only those courts have acquired any significant familiarity with the issues. The treaty contemplates that in a federal system like ours, there could be a "central authority" implementing the treaty in each state and a "central central authority" for the federation. That central authority might be the U.S. Justice Department, which already serves as central authority under some similar international conventions, or another federal agency such as the Department of Health and Human Services.

The meetings resulting in the final text, in which some 27 countries participated, were held in the Netherlands October 6-12, 1980.

## CONVENTION SUMMARIZED

It begins with a statement of purpose: to secure the prompt return of children wrongfully removed or retained across international borders, and "to secure in all contracting states the effective enjoyment" of the rights of custody and visitation ("access"). There follows a statement of when the removal or retention of a child is considered wrongful: i.e., when it is in breach of custody rights being actually exercised by a person—or an institution—jointly or alone, "based on the law of the state in which the child was habitually resident immediately before the removal or retention." This includes not just custody under decrees, separation agreements or administrative decisions, but also the natural and assumed custody rights that a parent has before the matter has been brought to any courts' attention.

The convention's rules apply to any child under 16 who is habitually resident immediately before the breach of custody or visitation rights. Thus it would apply to one parent's decision to return with the (married or unmarried) couple's children to a state that is their native country and long-term residence and has strong claims to being their home state.

The convention requires contracting states to designate a "central authority" to discharge the duties imposed by the convention. It contemplates that federal states like the U.S. will let each member state appoint central authorities, but also appoint a federal central authority through which dealings with other countries can be channeled. These central authorities are required to take steps to discover the whereabouts of wrongfully removed or retained children, exchange information on the social background of the child for custody determinations, take all appropriate steps to bring about a voluntary resolution of the dispute, and when that fails "initiate or facilitate" judicial or administrative proceedings to return the child and, "where appropriate" determine the custody and visitation rights issues. It also requires legal aid in all appropriate cases, including services of lawyer counsel.

## TRIGGERING THE PROCESS

For the return of children, the convention sets up a system not unlike the Uniform Reciprocal Enforcement of Support Act: the aggrieved person goes to the central authority in either the child's habitual residence or the foreign state with an application giving basic information about the child and the offending parent, and the grounds of the claim. That application "may" be accompanied by a certified copy of any relevant decision or agreement and by a certificate or sworn declaration from "a competent authority of the state of the child's habitual residence," or "a qualified person" about what the substantive law of that state on custody is.

The further specific requirement that the central authority undertake negotiation of a consensual return before initiating any legal proceedings (Article 9) is of course subject to criticism as a measure that would only tip the hand of the authorities to the great advantage of an unscrupulous fugitive parent. Article 10 requires that if the judicial and administrative authorities have not reached a decision within six weeks after receipt of the application they must state their reasons to the applicant and to the central authority of the requesting state. The substantive rule of Article 11 is that when a breach of custody rights is found the central authority must order the return of the child forthwith—unless six months or more has elapsed from the date of the breach. The same article provides, though, that when the child's location was unknown, that six-month period runs from the date of the discovery of the child—provided that the total period from the breach to the deadline cannot exceed one year.

A very controversial article provides, however, that the authorities are not bound to order the return of a child if the removing parent establishes that the applicant was not "actually exercising the custody rights or acting in good faith," or that there is a substantial risk that return would mean physical or psychological harm to the child or place the child in an "intolerable situation." The authority can also refuse return of a child who objects to return "and has attained an age and degree of maturity at which it is appropriate to take account of its views."

In all of this, the central authorities have to take into account ("have regard to") the law of the requesting state. Although they are not required to, the authorities can order the return of a child after the expiration of the deadlines. The convention specifically declares that a decision to return the child shall not be construed as a decision on the merits of a custody-rights dispute.

The visitation, or access, provision of the convention contemplates the handling of the application in the same way as the permanent return application. In these controversies, the central authorities (probably the Justice Department in U.S.) can themselves initiate legal processing to fix or protect the visitation rights.

## FINANCING THE PROCESS

Article 21 requires that foreign parents be afforded the same rights of legal aid in contracting states as citizens and residents of the state have. A very important provision requires that the central authorities bear all the costs of actions brought under this convention and impose no charges in relation to applications. They may, however, require the payment of charges by privately employed legal counsel voluntarily enlisted from outside the legal aid system, and the payment of actual travel expenses for repatriating a child.

A central authority is not required to accept an application that is obviously not well-founded, but when it so rejects an application it must immediately inform the applicant and the central authority of the applicant's state as to why there was a rejection. The convention ends with a statement that nothing in it prevents any person from bypassing the convention and the central authority in applying directly to the judicial or administrative authorities of a contracting country.

A major U.S. accomplishment was revision of the time limits specified for requesting action under the convention. There had been a six-month time limit, with an additional six months available for cases in which the child could not be found. At U.S. insistence a one-year time limit for all cases was adopted. Also accepted was a German proposal that a child would still be returned even though proceedings were initiated after one year, unless the abductor established that the child was integrated into the new environment. Both these changes should keep the rules from encouraging abducting parents to move about and hide the children while time limits run.

The conferees turned down a proposal to let countries require courts of the habitual residence country to produce a ruling on wrongfulness of the removal of the child as a precondition to ordering the child's return. The language adopted simply allows courts in the second country to ask the habitual residence country's courts for such a ruling.

Article 16 should keep a "race to the court house" from being the ultimate determinant of a child's custody. Though the child-snatcher often seeks to legitimize his custody in the courts of the new country, this article requires any court that has received notice of a child's unauthorized international removal to suspend such proceedings until the case has been processed under the convention.

The United States argued strenuously against the drafters' earlier decision to require national "central authorities" to provide free legal services to all litigants under this convention. It even took the position that this requirement would make it impossible for the United States to ratify. A compromise resulted in a text that allows certain countries to sign with a "reservation" excluding this aspect of the agreement.

## *THE STRASBOURG CONVENTION*

The Council of Europe's Strasbourg Convention, known as the European Convention on Recognition and Enforcement of Decisions Concerning Custody of Children and on Restoration of Custody of Children, is included because of the great difficulty American attorneys are likely to have obtaining a copy elsewhere, even though the chances of its usefulness in an American custody case are not great. The convention, signed by 15 countries in May of 1980, applies only between the 21 European nations that make up the Council of Europe.

The United States, Canada, Australia, and other non-European countries could not become signatories to this convention even if they wanted to. However, it could be very useful in securing return of a child through the Hague convention if a child has been taken from the United States to another country such as Great Britian, which has membership in both conventions, and thence to a Strasbourg-only country such as Italy or West Germany.

Though persons close to the negotiation process have tended to make much of the difference between the Hague and Strasbourg conventions, they do not loom so large to the lay person. The concepts and mechansims are substantially alike. The Strasbourg convention aims at swift, summary and inexpensive return of children, and requires every country to provide free and expeditious tracing of missing children and to recognize other signatories' custody orders. It proposes an intermediate organization in each country which will return a child who was "improperly removed" if the request is made within six months. Austria, Belgium, the U.K., Cyprus, France, West Germany, Greece, Italy, Ireland, Liechtenstein, Luxembourg, The Netherlands, Portugal, Spain and Switzerland have signed the convention so far.

# TEXT OF THE HAGUE CONVENTION

*Final Act of the Fourteenth Session*

The undersigned, Delegates of the Governments of Argentina, Australia, Austria, Belgium, Canada, Czechoslovakia, Denmark, the Arab Republic of Egypt, Finland, France, the Federal Republic of Germany, Greece, Ireland, Israel, Italy, Japan, Jugoslavia, Luxemburg, the Netherlands, Norway, Portugal, Spain, Surinam, Sweden, Switzerland, Turkey, the United Kingdom of Great Britain and Northern Ireland, the United States of America and Venezuela, and the Representatives of the Governments of Brazil, the Holy See, Hungary, Monaco, Morocco, the Union of Soviet Socialist Republics and Uruguay participating by invitation or as Observer, convened at The Hague on the 6th October 1980, at the invitation of the Government of the Netherlands, in the Fourteenth Session of the Hague Conference on Private International Law.

Following the deliberations laid down in the records of the meetings, have decided to submit to their Governments –

**The following draft Convention—**

CONVENTION ON THE CIVIL ASPECTS OF INTERNATIONAL CHILD ABDUCTION

The States signatory to the present Convention,

Firmly convinced that the interests of children are of paramount importance in matters relating to their custody,

Desiring to protect children internationally from the harmful effects of their wrongful removal or retention and to establish procedures to ensure their prompt return to the State of their habitual residence, as well as to secure protection for rights of access,

Have resolved to conclude a Convention to this effect, and have agreed upon the following provisions –

## CHAPTER I – SCOPE OF THE CONVENTION

### *Article 1*

The objects of the present Convention are:

*a* to secure the prompt return of children wrongfully removed to or retained in any Contracting State; and

b to ensure that rights of custody and of access under the law of one Contracting State are effectively respected in the other Contracting States.

### *Article 2*

Contracting States shall take all appropriate measures to secure within their territories the implementation of the objects of the Convention. For this purpose they shall use the most expeditious procedures available.

### *Article 3*

The removal or the retention of a child is to be considered wrongful where:

*a* it is in breach of rights of custody attributed to a person, an institution or any other body, either jointly or alone, under the law of the State in which the child was habitually resident immediately before the removal or retention; and

*b* at the time of removal or retention those rights were actually exercised, either jointly or alone, or would have been so exercised but for the removal or retention.

The rights of custody mentioned in sub-paragraph *a* above, may arise in particular by operation of law or by reason of a judicial or administrative decision, or by reason of an agreement having legal effect under the law of that State.

*Article 4*

The Convention shall apply to any child who was habitually resident in a Contracting State immediately before any breach of custody or access rights. The Convention shall cease to apply when the child attains the age of 16 years.

*Article 5*

For the purposes of this Convention:

*a* 'rights of custody' shall include rights relating to the care of the person of the child and, in particular, the right to determine the child's place of residence;

*b* 'rights of access' shall include the right to take a child for a limited period of time to a place other than the child's habitual residence.

## CHAPTER II – CENTRAL AUTHORITIES

*Article 6*

A Contracting State shall designate a Central Authority to discharge the duties which are imposed by the Convention upon such authorities.
Federal States, States with more than one system of law or States having autonomous territorial organizations shall be free to appoint more than one Central Authority and to specify the territorial extent of their powers. Where a State has appointed more than one Central Authority, it shall designate the Central Authority to which applications may be addressed for transmission to the appropriate Central Authority within that State.

*Article 7*

Central Authorities shall co-operate with each other and promote co-operation amongst the competent authorities in their respective States to secure the prompt return of children and to achieve the other objects of this Convention.

In particular, either directly or through any intermediary, they shall take all appropriate measures –

*a* to discover the whereabouts of a child who has been wrongfully removed or retained;

*b* to prevent further harm to the child or prejudice to interested parties by taking or causing to be taken provisional measures;

*c* to secure the voluntary return of the child or to bring about an amicable resolution of the issues;

*d* to exchange, where desirable, information relating to the social background of the child;

*e* to provide information of a general character as to the law of their State in connection with the application of the Convention;

*f* to initiate or facilitate the institution of judicial or administrative proceedings with a view to obtaining the return of the child and, in a proper case, to make arrangements for organizing or securing the effective exercise of rights of access;

*g* where the circumstances so require, to provide or facilitate the provision of legal aid and advice, including the participation of legal counsel and advisers;

*h* to provide such administrative arrangements as may be necessary and appropriate to secure the safe return of the child;

*i* to keep each other informed with respect to the operation of this Convention and, as far as possible, to eliminate any obstacles to its application.

## CHAPTER III – RETURN OF CHILDREN

### *Article 8*

Any person, institution or other body claiming that a child has been removed or retained in breach of custody rights may apply either to the Central Authority of the child's habitual residence or to the Central Authority of any other Contracting State for assistance in securing the return of the child.

The application shall contain –

*a* information concerning the identity of the applicant, of the child and of the person alleged to have removed or retained the child;

*b* where available, the date of birth of the child;

*c* the grounds on which the applicant's claim for return of the child is based;

*d* all available information relating to the whereabouts of the child and the identity of the person with whom the child is presumed to be.

The application may be accompanied or supplemented by –

*e* an authenticated copy of any relevant decision or agreement;

*f* a certificate or an affidavit emanating from a Central Authority, or other competent authority of the State of the child's habitual residence, or from a qualified person, concerning the relevant law of that State;

*g* any other relevant document.

*Article 9*

If the Central Authority which receives an application referred to in Article 8 has reason to believe that the child is in another Contracting State, it shall directly and without delay transmit the application to the Central Authority of that Contracting State and inform the requesting Central Authority, or the applicant, as the case may be.

*Article 10*

The Central Authority of the State where the child is shall take or cause to be taken all appropriate measures in order to obtain the voluntary return of the child.

*Article 11*

The judicial or administrative authorities of Contracting States shall act expeditiously in proceedings for the return of children.

If the judicial or administrative authority concerned has not reached a decision within six weeks from the date of commencement of the proceedings, the applicant or the Central Authority of the requested State, on its own initiative or if asked by the Central Authority of the requesting State, shall have the right to request a statement of the reasons for the delay. If a reply is received by the Central Authority of the requested State, that Authority shall transmit the reply to the Central Authority of the requesting State, or to the applicant, as the case may be.

*Article 12*

Where a child has been wrongfully removed or retained in terms of Article 3 and, at the date of the commencement of the proceedings before the judicial or administrative authority of the Contracting State where the child is, a period of less than one year has elapsed from the date of the wrongful removal or retention, the authority concerned shall order the return of the child forthwith.

The judicial or administrative authority, even where the proceedings have been commenced after the expiration of the period of one year referred to in the preceding paragraph, shall also order the return of the child, unless it is demonstrated that the child is now settled in its new environment.

Where the judicial or administrative authority in the requested State has reason to believe that the child has been taken to another State, it may stay the proceedings or dismiss the application for the return of the child.

*Article 13*

Notwithstanding the provisions of the preceding Article, the judicial or administrative authority of the requested State is not bound to order the return of the child if the person, institution or other body which opposes its return establishes that:

*a* the person, institution or other body having the care of the person of the child was not actually exercising the custody rights at the time of removal or retention, or had consented to or subsequently acquiesced in the removal or retention; or

*b* there is a grave risk that his or her return would expose the child to physical or psychological harm or otherwise place the child in an intolerable situation.

The judicial or administrative authority may also refuse to order the return of the child if it finds that the child objects to being returned and has attained an age and degree of maturity at which it is appropriate to take account of its views.

In considering the circumstances referred to in this Article, the judicial and administrative authorities shall take into account the information relating to the social background of the child provided by the Central Authority or other competent authority of the child's habitual residence.

### *Article 14*

In ascertaining whether there has been a wrongful removal or retention within the meaning of Article 3, the judicial or administrative authorities of the requested State may take notice directly of the law of, and of judicial or administrative decisions, formally recognized or not in the State of the habitual residence of the child without recourse to the specific procedures for the proof of that law or for the recognition of foreign decisions which would otherwise be applicable.

### *Article 15*

The judicial or administrative authorities of a Contracting State may, prior to the making of an order for the return of the child, request that the applicant obtain from the authorities of the State of the habitual residence of the child a decision or other determination that the removal or retention was wrongful within the meaning of Article 3 of the Convention, where such a decision or determination may be obtained in that State. The Central Authorities of the Contracting States shall so far as practicable assist applicants to obtain such a decision or determination.

*Article 16*

After receiving notice of a wrongful removal or retention of a child in the sense of Article 3, the judicial or administrative authorities of the Contracting State to which the child has been removed or in which it has been retained shall not decide on the merits of rights of custody until it has been determined that the child is not to be returned under this Convention or unless an application under this Convention is not lodged within a reasonable time following receipt of the notice.

*Article 17*

The sole fact that a decision relating to custody has been given in or is entitled to recognition in the requested State shall not be a ground for refusing to return a child under this Convention, but the judicial or administrative authorities of the requested State may take account of the reasons for that decision in applying this Convention.

*Article 18*

The provisions of this Chapter do not limit the power of a judicial or administrative authority to order the return of the child at any time.

*Article 19*

A decision under this Convention concerning the return of the child shall not to be taken to be a determination on the merits of any custody issue.

*Article 20*

The return of the child under the provisions of Article 12 may be refused if this would not be permitted by the fundamental principles of the requested State relating to the protection of human rights and fundamental freedoms.

## CHAPTER IV – RIGHTS OF ACCESS

### *Article 21*

An application to make arrangements for organizing or securing the effective exercise of rights of access may be presented to the Central Authorities of the Contracting States in the same way as an application for the return of a child.

The Central Authorities are bound by the obligations of co-operation which are set forth in Article 7 to promote the peaceful enjoyment of access rights and the fulfilment of any conditions to which the exercise of those rights may be subject. The Central Authorities shall take steps to remove, as far as possible, all obstacles to the exercise of such rights.

The Central Authorities, either directly or through intermediaries, may initiate or assist in the institution of proceedings with a view to organizing or protecting these rights and securing respect for the conditions to which the exercise of these rights may be subject.

## CHAPTER V – GENERAL PROVISIONS

### *Article 22*

No security, bond or deposit, however described, shall be required to guarantee the payment of costs and expenses in the judicial or administrative proceedings falling within the scope of this Convention.

### *Article 23*

No legalization or similar formality may be required in the context of this Convention.

### *Article 24*

Any application, communication or other document sent to the Central Authority of the requested State shall be in the original language, and shall be accompanied by a

translation into the official language or one of the official languages of the requested State or, where that is not feasible, a translation into French or English.
However, a Contracting State may, by making a reservation in accordance with Article 42, object to the use of either French or English, but not both, in any application, communication or other document sent to its Central Authority.

*Article 25*

Nationals of the Contracting States and persons who are habitually resident within those States shall be entitled in matters concerned with the application of this Convention to legal aid and advice in any other Contracting State on the same conditions as if they themselves were nationals of and habitually resident in that State.

*Article 26*

Each Central Authority shall bear its own costs in applying this Convention.
Central Authorities and other public services of Contracting States shall not impose any charges in relation to applications submitted under this Convention. In particular, they may not require any payment from the applicant towards the costs and expenses of the proceedings or, where applicable, those arising from the participation of legal counsel or advisers. However, they may require the payment of the expenses incurred or to be incurred in implementing the return of the child.
However, a Contracting State may, by making a reservation in accordance with Article 42, declare that it shall not be bound to assume any costs referred to in the preceding paragraph resulting from the participation of legal counsel or advisers or from court proceedings, except insofar as those costs may be covered by its system of legal aid and advice.
Upon ordering the return of a child or issuing an order concerning rights of access under this Convention, the judicial or administrative authorities may, where appropriate, direct the person who removed or retained

the child, or who prevented the exercise of rights of access, to pay necessary expenses incurred by or on behalf of the applicant, including travel expenses, any costs incurred or payments made for locating the child, the costs of legal representation of the applicant, and those of returning the child.

*Article 27*

When it is manifest that the requirements of this Convention are not fulfilled or that the application is otherwise not well founded, a Central Authority is not bound to accept the application. In that case, the Central Authority shall forthwith inform the applicant or the Central Authority through which the application was submitted, as the case may be, of its reasons.

*Article 28*

A Central Authority may require that the application be accompanied by a written authorization empowering it to act on behalf of the applicant, or to designate a representative so to act.

*Article 29*

This Convention shall not preclude any person, institution or body who claims that there has been a breach of custody or access rights within the meaning of Article 3 or 21 from applying directly to the judicial or administrative authorities of a Contracting State, whether or not under the provisions of this Convention.

*Article 30*

Any application submitted to the Central Authorities or directly to the judicial or administrative authorities of a Contracting State in accordance with the terms of this Convention, together with documents and any other information appended thereto or provided by a Central Authority, shall be admissible in the courts or administrative authorities of the Contracting States.

*Article 31*

In relation to a State which in matters of custody of children has two or more systems of law applicable in different territorial units –

*a* any reference to habitual residence in that State shall be construed as referring to habitual residence in a territorial unit of that State;

*b* any reference to the law of the State of habitual residence shall be construed as referring to the law of the territorial unit in that State where the child habitually resides.

*Article 32*

In relation to a State which in matters of custody of children has two or more systems of law applicable to different categories of persons, any reference to the law of that State shall be construed as referring to the legal system specified by the law of that State.

*Article 33*

A State within which different territorial units have their own rules of law in respect of custody of children shall not be bound to apply this Convention where a State with a unified system of law would not be bound to do so.

*Article 34*

This Convention shall take priority in matters within its scope over the *Convention of 5 October 1961 concerning the powers of authorities and the law applicable in respect of the protection of minors*, as between Parties to both Conventions. Otherwise the present Convention shall not restrict the application of an international instrument in force between the State of origin and the State addressed or other law of the State addressed for the purposes of obtaining the return of a child who has been wrongfully removed or retained or of organizing access rights.

*Article 35*

This Convention shall apply as between Contracting States only to wrongful removals or retentions occurring after its entry into force in those States.
Where a declaration has been made under Article 39 or 40 the reference in the preceding paragraph to a Contracting State shall be taken to refer to the territorial unit or units in relation to which this Convention applies.

*Article 36*

Nothing in this Convention shall prevent two or more Contracting States, in order to limit the restrictions to which the return of the child may be subject, from agreeing among themselves to derogate from any provisions of this Convention which may imply such a restriction.

## CHAPTER VI – FINAL CLAUSES

*Article 37*

The Convention shall be open for signature by the States which were Members of the Hague Conference on Private International Law at the time of its Fourteenth Session.
It shall be ratified, accepted or approved and the instruments of ratification, acceptance or approval shall be deposited with the Ministry of Foreign Affairs of the Kingdom of the Netherlands.

*Article 38*

Any other State may accede to the Convention.
The instrument of accession shall be deposited with the Ministry of Foreign Affairs of the Kingdom of the Netherlands.
The Convention shall enter into force for a State acceding to it on the first day of the third calendar month after the deposit of its instrument of accession.
The accession will have effect only as regards the relations between the acceding State and such Contracting States as will have declared their acceptance of the

accession. Such a declaration will also have to be made by any Member State ratifying, accepting or approving the Convention after an accession. Such declaration shall be deposited at the Ministry of Foreign Affairs of the Kingdom of the Netherlands; this Ministry shall forward, through diplomatic channels, a certified copy to each of the Contracting States.
The Convention will enter into force as between the acceding State and the State that has declared its acceptance of the accession on the first day of the third calendar month after the deposit of the declaration of acceptance.

*Article 39*

Any State may, at the time of signature, ratification, acceptance, approval or accession, declare that the Convention shall extend to all the territories for the international relations of which it is responsible, or to one or more of them. Such a declaration shall take effect at the time the Convention enters into force for that State.
Such declaration, as well as any subsequent extension, shall be notified to the Ministry of Foreign Affairs of the Kingdom of the Netherlands.

*Article 40*

If a Contracting State has two or more territorial units in which different systems of law are applicable in relation to matters dealt with in this Convention, it may at the time of signature, ratification, acceptance, approval or accession declare that this Convention shall extend to all its territorial units or only to one or more of them and may modify this declaration by submitting another declaration at any time. Any such declaration shall be notified to the Ministry of Foreign Affairs of the Kingdom of the Netherlands and shall state expressly the territorial units to which the Convention applies.

*Article 41*

Where a Contracting State has a system of government under which executive, judicial and legislative powers are distributed between central and other authorities within that State, its signature or ratification, acceptance or approval of, or accession to this Convention, or its making of any declaration in terms of Article 40 shall carry no implication as to the internal distribution of powers within that State.

*Article 42*

Any State may, not later than the time of ratification, acceptance, approval or accession, or at the time of making a declaration in terms of Article 39 or 40, make one or both of the reservations provided for in Article 24 and Article 26, third paragraph. No other reservation shall be permitted.
Any State may at any time withdraw a reservation it has made. The withdrawal shall be notified to the Ministry of Foreign Affairs of the Kingdom of the Netherlands.
The reservation shall cease to have effect on the first day of the third calendar month after the notification referred to in the preceding paragraph.

*Article 43*

The Convention shall enter into force on the first day of the third calendar month after the deposit of the third instrument of ratification, acceptance, approval or accession referred to in Articles 37 and 38.
Thereafter the Convention shall enter into force –

1 for each State ratifying, accepting, approving or acceding to it subsequently, on the first day of the third calendar month after the deposit of its instrument of ratification, acceptance, approval or accession;

2 for any territory or territorial unit to which the Convention has been extended in conformity with Article 39 or 40, on the first day of the third calendar month after the notification referred to in that Article.

*Article 44*

The Convention shall remain in force for five years from the date of its entry into force in accordance with the first paragraph of Article 43 even for States which subsequently have ratified, accepted, approved it or acceded to it.

If there has been no denunciation, it shall be renewed tacitly every five years.

Any denunciation shall be notified to the Ministry of Foreign Affairs of the Kingdom of the Netherlands at least six months before the expiry of the five year period. It may be limited to certain of the territories or territorial units to which the Convention applies.

The denunciation shall have effect only as regards the State which has notified it. The Convention shall remain in force for the other Contracting States.

*Article 45*

The Ministry of Foreign Affairs of the Kingdom of the Netherlands shall notify the States Members of the Conference, and the States which have acceded in accordance with Article 38, of the following –

1 the signatures and ratifications, acceptances and approvals referred to in Article 37;

2 the accessions referred to in Article 38;

3 the date on which the Convention enters into force in accordance with Article 43;

4 the extensions referred to in Article 39;

5 the declarations referred to in Articles 38 and 40;

6 the reservations referred to in Article 24 and Article 26, third paragraph, and the withdrawals referred to in Article 42;

7 the denunciations referred to in Article 44.

In witness whereof the undersigned, being duly authorized thereto, have signed this Convention.

Done at The Hague, on the .... day of .... 19..., in the English and French languages, both texts being equally authentic, in a single copy which shall be deposited in the archives of the Government of the Kingdom of the Netherlands, and of which a certified copy shall be sent, through diplomatic channels, to each of the States Members of the Hague Conference on Private International Law at the date of its Fourteenth Session.

# TEXT OF THE STRASBOURG CONVENTION

## TEXT OF THE EUROPEAN CONVENTION ON RECOGNITION AND ENFORCEMENT OF DECISIONS CONCERNING CUSTODY OF CHILDREN AND ON RESTORATION OF CUSTODY OF CHILDREN

The member States of the Council of Europe, signatory hereto,

Recognising that in the member States of the Council of Europe the welfare of the child is of overriding importance in reaching decisions concerning his custody;

Considering that the making of arrangements to ensure that decisions concerning the custody of a child can be more widely recognised and enforced will provide greater protection of the welfare of children;

Considering it desirable, with this end in view, to emphasise that the right of access of parents is a normal corollary to the right of custody;

Noting the increasing number of cases where children have been improperly removed across an international frontier and the difficulties of securing adequate solutions to the problems caused by such cases;

Desirous of making suitable provision to enable the custody of children which has been arbitrarily interrupted to be restored;

Convinced of the desirability of making arrangements for this purpose answering to different needs and different circumstances;

Desiring to establish legal co-operation between their authorities,

Have agreed as follows:

### Article 1

For the purpose of this Convention:

a. *child* means a person of any nationality, so long as he is under 16 years of age and has not the right to decide on his own place of residence under the law of his habitual residence, the law of his nationality or the internal law of the State addressed;

b. *authority* means a judicial or administrative authority;

c. *decision relating to custody* means a decision of an authority in so far as it relates to the care of the person of the child, including the right to decide on the place of his residence, or to the right of access to him;

d. *improper removal* means the removal of a child across an international frontier in breach of a decision relating to his custody which has been given in a Contracting State and which is enforceable in such a State; improper removal also includes:

i. the failure to return a child across an international frontier at the end of a period of the exercise of the right of access to this child or at the end of any other temporary stay in a territory other than that, where the custody is exercised;

ii. a removal which is subsequently declared unlawful within the meaning of Article 12.

## PART 1

### *Central authorities*

#### Article 2

1. Each Contracting State shall appoint a central authority to carry out the functions provided for by this Convention.

2. Federal States and States with more than one legal system shall be free to appoint more than one central authority and shall determine the extent of their competence.

3. The Secretary General of the Council of Europe shall be notified of any appointment under this Article.

#### Article 3

1. The central authorities of the Contracting States shall co-operate with each other and promote co-operation between the competent authorities in their respective countries. They shall act with all necessary despatch.

2. With a view to facilitating the operation of this Convention, the central authorities of the Contracting States:

*a.* shall secure the transmission of requests for information coming from competent authorities and relating to legal or factual matters concerning pending proceedings;

*b.* shall provide each other on request with information about their law relating to the custody of children and any changes in that law;

*c.* shall keep each other informed of any difficulties likely to arise in applying the Convention and, as far as possible, eliminate obstacles to its application.

## Article 4

1. Any person who has obtained in a Contracting State a decision relating to the custody of a child and who wishes to have that decision recognised or enforced in another Contracting State may submit an application for this purpose to the central authority in any Contracting State.

2. The application shall be accompanied by the documents mentioned in Article 13.

3. The central authority receiving the application, if it is not the central authority in the State addressed, shall send the documents directly and without delay to that central authority.

4. The central authority receiving the application may refuse to intervene where it is manifestly clear that the conditions laid down by this Convention are not satisfied.

5. The central authority receiving the application shall keep the applicant informed without delay of the progress of his application.

## Article 5

1. The central authority in the State addressed shall take or cause to be taken without delay all steps which it considers to be appropriate, if necessary by instituting proceedings before its competent authorities, in order:

*a.* to discover the whereabouts of the child;

*b.* to avoid, in particular by any necessary provisional measures, prejudice to the interests of the child or of the applicant;

*c.* to secure the recognition or enforcement of the decision;

*d.* to secure the delivery of the child to the applicant where enforcement is granted;

*e.* to inform the requesting authority of the measures taken and their results.

2. Where the central authority in the State addressed has reason to believe that the child is in the territory of another Contracting State it shall send the documents directly and without delay to the central authority of that State.

3. With the exception of the cost of repatriation, each Contracting State undertakes not to claim any payment from an applicant in respect of any measures taken under paragraph 1 of this Article by the central authority of that State on the applicant's behalf, including the costs of proceedings and, where applicable, the costs incurred by the assistance of a lawyer.

4. If recognition or enforcement is refused, and if the central authority of the State addressed considers that it should comply with a request by the applicant to bring in that State proceedings concerning the substance of the case, that authority shall use its best endeavours to secure the representation of the applicant in the proceedings under conditions no less favourable than those available to a person who is resident in and a national of that State and for this purpose it may, in particular, institute proceedings before its competent authorities.

## Article 6

1. Subject to any special agreements made between the central authorities concerned and to the provisions of paragraph 3 of this Article:

*a.* communications to the central authority of the State addressed shall be made in the official language or in one of the official languages of that State or be accompanied by a translation into that language;

*b.* the central authority of the State addressed shall nevertheless accept communications made in English or in French or accompanied by a translation into one of these languages.

2. Communications coming from the central authority of the State addressed, including the results of enquiries carried out, may be made in the official language or one of the official languages of that State or in English or French.

3. A Contracting State may exclude wholly or partly the provisions of paragraph 1.*b* of this Article. When a Contracting State has made this reservation any other Contracting State may also apply the reservation in respect of that State.

## PART II

### *Recognition and enforcement of decisions and restoration of custody of children*

#### Article 7

A decision relating to custody given in a Contracting State shall be recognised and, where it is enforceable in the State of origin, made enforceable in every other Contracting State.

#### Article 8

1. In the case of an improper removal, the central authority of the State addressed shall cause steps to be taken forthwith to restore the custody of the child where:

*a.* at the time of the institution of the proceedings in the State where the decision was given or at the time of the improper removal, if earlier, the child and his parents had as their sole nationality the nationality of that State and the child had his habitual residence in the territory of that State, and

*b.* a request for the restoration was made to a central authority within a period of six months from the date of the improper removal.

2. If, in accordance with the law of the State addressed, the requirements of paragraph 1 of this Article cannot be complied with without recourse to a judicial authority, none of the grounds of refusal specified in this Convention shall apply to the judicial proceedings.

3. Where there is an agreement officially confirmed by a competent authority between the person having the custody of the child and another person to allow the other person a right of access, and the child, having been taken abroad, has not been restored at the end of the agreed period to the person having the custody, custody of the child shall be restored in accordance with paragraphs 1.*b* and 2 of this Article. The same shall apply in the case of a decision of the competent authority granting such a right to a person who has not the custody of the child.

#### Article 9

1. In cases of improper removal, other than those dealt with in Article 8, in which an application has been made to a central authority within a period of six months from the date of the removal, recognition and enforcement may be refused only if:

*a.* in the case of a decision given in the absence of the defendant or his legal representative, the defendant was not duly served with the document which instituted the proceedings or an equivalent document in sufficient time to enable him to arrange his defence; but such a failure to effect service cannot constitute a ground for refusing recognition or enforcement where service was not effected because the defendant had concealed his whereabouts from the person who instituted the proceedings in the State of origin;

*b.* in the case of a decision given in the absence of the defendant or his legal representative, the competence of the authority giving the decision was not founded:

i. on the habitual residence of the defendant, or

ii. on the last common habitual residence of the child's parents, at least one parent being still habitually resident there, or

iii. on the habitual residence of the child;

*c.* the decision is incompatible with a decision relating to custody which became enforceable in the State addressed before the removal of the child, unless the child has had his habitual residence in the territory of the requesting State for one year before his removal.

2. Where no application has been made to a central authority, the provisions of paragraph 1 of this Article shall apply equally, if recognition and enforcement are requested within six months from the date of the improper removal.

3. In no circumstances may the foreign decision be reviewed as to its substance.

## Article 10

1. In cases other than those covered by Articles 8 and 9, recognition and enforcement may be refused not only on the grounds provided for in Article 9 but also on any of the following grounds:

*a.* if it is found that the effects of the decision are manifestly incompatible with the fundamental principles of the law relating to the family and children in the State addressed;

*b.* if it is found that by reason of a change in the circumstances including the passage of time but not including a mere change in the residence of the child after an improper removal, the effects of the original decision are manifestly no longer in accordance with the welfare of the child;

*c.* if at the time when the proceedings were instituted in the State of origin:

i. the child was a national of the State addressed or was habitually resident there and no such connection existed with the State of origin;

ii. the child was a national both of the State of origin and of the State addressed and was habitually resident in the State addressed;

*d.* if the decision is incompatible with a decision given in the State addressed or enforceable in that State after being given in a third State, pursuant to proceedings begun before the submission of the request for recognition or enforcement, and if the refusal is in accordance with the welfare of the child.

2. In the same cases, proceedings for recognition or enforcement may be adjourned on any of the following grounds:

*a.* if an ordinary form of review of the original decision has been commenced;

*b.* if proceedings relating to the custody of the child, commenced before the proceedings in the State of origin were instituted, are pending in the State addressed;

c. if another decision concerning the custody of the child is the subject of proceedings for enforcement or of any other proceedings concerning the recognition of the decision.

### Article 11

1. Decisions on rights of access and provisions of decisions relating to custody which deal with the right of access shall be recognised and enforced subject to the same conditions as other decisions relating to custody.

2. However, the competent authority of the State addressed may fix the conditions for the implementation and exercise of the right of access taking into account, in particular, undertakings given by the parties on this matter.

3. Where no decision on the right of access has been taken or where recognition or enforcement of the decision relating to custody is refused, the central authority of the State addressed may apply to its competent authorities for a decision on the right of access, if the person claiming a right of access so requests.

### Article 12

Where, at the time of the removal of a child across an international frontier, there is no enforceable decision given in a Contracting State relating to his custody, the provisions of this Convention shall apply to any subsequent decision, relating to the custody of that child and declaring the removal to be unlawful, given in a Contracting State at the request of any interested person.

## PART III

### *Procedure*

### Article 13

1. A request for recognition or enforcement in another Contracting State of a decision relating to custody shall be accompanied by:

*a.* a document authorising the central authority of the State addressed to act on behalf of the applicant or to designate another representative for that purpose;

*b.* a copy of the decision which satisfies the necessary conditions of authenticity;

*c.* in the case of a decision given in the absence of the defendant or his legal representative, a document which establishes that the defendant was duly served with the document which instituted the proceedings or an equivalent document;

*d.* if applicable, any document which establishes that, in accordance with the law of the State of origin, the decision is enforceable;

*e.* if possible, a statement indicating the whereabouts or likely whereabouts of the child in the State addressed;

*f.* proposals as to how the custody of the child should be restored.

2. The documents mentioned above shall, where necessary, be accompanied by a translation according to the provisions laid down in Article 6.

### Article 14

Each Contracting State shall apply a simple and expeditious procedure for recognition and enforcement of decisions relating to the custody of a child. To that end it shall ensure that a request for enforcement may be lodged by simple application.

### Article 15

1. Before reaching a decision under paragraph 1.*b* of Article 10, the authority concerned in the State addressed:

*a.* shall ascertain the child's views unless this is impracticable having regard in particular to his age and understanding; and

*b.* may request that any appropriate enquiries be carried out.

2. The cost of enquiries in any Contracting State shall be met by the authorities of the State where they are carried out.

Requests for enquiries and the results of enquiries may be sent to the authority concerned through the central authorities.

### Article 16

For the purposes of this Convention, no legalisation or any like formality may be required.

## PART IV

### *Reservations*

### Article 17

1. A Contracting State may make a reservation that, in cases covered by Articles 8 and 9 or either of these Articles, recognition and enforcement of decisions relating to custody may be refused on such of the grounds provided under Article 10 as may be specified in the reservation.

2. Recognition and enforcement of decisions given in a Contracting State which has made the reservation provided for in paragraph 1 of this Article may be refused in any other Contracting State on any of the additional grounds referred to in that reservation.

### Article 18

A Contracting State may make a reservation that it shall not be bound by the provisions of Article 12. The provisions of this Convention shall not apply to decisions referred to in Article 12 which have been given in a Contracting State which has made such a reservation.

## PART V

### *Other Instruments*

### Article 19

This Convention shall not exclude the possibility of relying on any other international instrument in force between the State of origin and the State addressed or on any other law of the State addressed not derived from an international agreement for the purpose of obtaining recognition or enforcement of a decision.

Article 20

1. This Convention shall not affect any obligations which a Contracting State may have towards a non-contracting State under an international instrument dealing with matters governed by this Convention.

2. When two or more Contracting States have enacted uniform laws in relation to custody of children or created a special system of recognition or enforcement of decisions in this field, or if they should do so in the future, they shall be free to apply, between themselves, those laws or that system in place of this Convention or any part of it. In order to avail themselves of this provision the States shall notify their decision to the Secretary General of the Council of Europe. Any alteration or revocation of this decision must also be notified.

## PART VI

*Final clauses*

Article 21

This Convention shall be open for signature by the member States of the Council of Europe. It is subject to ratification, acceptance or approval. Instruments of ratification, acceptance or approval shall be deposited with the Secretary General of the Council of Europe.

Article 22

1. This Convention shall enter into force on the first day of the month following the expiration of a period of three months after the date on which three member States of the Council of Europe have expressed their consent to be bound by the Convention in accordance with the provisions of Article 21.

2. In respect of any member State which subsequently expresses its consent to be bound by it, the Convention shall enter into force on the first day of the month following the expiration of a period of three months after the date of the deposit of the instrument of ratification, acceptance or approval.

Article 23

1. After the entry into force of this Convention, the Committee of Ministers of the Council of Europe may invite any State not a member

of the Council to accede to this Convention, by a decision taken by the majority provided for by Article 20.*d* of the Statute and by the unanimous vote of the representatives of the Contracting States entitled to sit on the Committee.

2. In respect of any acceding State, the Convention shall enter into force on the first day of the month following he expiration of a period of three months after the date of deposit of the instrument of accession with the Secretary General of the Council of Europe.

## Article 24

1. Any State may at the time of signature or when depositing its instrument of ratification, acceptance, approval or accession, specify the territory or territories to which this Convention shall apply.

2. Any State may at any later date, by a declaration addressed to the Secretary General of the Council of Europe, extend the application of this Convention to any other territory specified in the declaration. In respect of such territory, the Convention shall enter into force on the first day of the month following the expiration of a period of three months after the date of receipt by the Secretary General of such declaration.

3. Any declaration made under the two preceding paragraphs may, in respect of any territory specified in such declaration, be withdrawn by a notification addressed to the Secretary General. The withdrawal shall become effective on the first day of the month following the expiration of a period of six months after the date of receipt of such notification by the Secretary General.

## Article 25

1. A State which has two or more territorial units in which different systems of law apply in matters of custody of children and of recognition and enforcement of decisions relating to custody may, at the time of signature or when depositing its instrument of ratification, acceptance, approval or accession, declare that this Convention shall apply to all its territorial units or to one or more of them.

2. Such a State may at any later date, by a declaration addressed to the Secretary General of the Council of Europe, extend the application of this Convention to any other territorial unit specified in the declaration. In respect of such territorial unit the Convention shall enter into force on the first day of the month following the expiration of a period of three months after the date of receipt by the Secretary General of such declaration.

3. Any declaration made under the two preceding paragraphs may, in respect of any territorial unit specified in such declaration, be withdrawn by notification addressed to the Secretary General. The withdrawal shall become effective on the first day of the month following the expiration of a period of six months after the date of receipt of such notification by the Secretary General.

### Article 26

1. In relation to a State which has in matters of custody two or more systems of law of territorial application:

*a.* reference to the law of a person's habitual residence or to the law of a person's nationality shall be construed as referring to the system of law determined by the rules in force in that State or, if there are no such rules, to the system of law with which the person concerned is most closely connected;

*b.* reference to the State of origin or to the State addressed shall be construed as referring, as the case may be, to the territorial unit where the decision was given or to the territorial unit where recognition or enforcement of the decision or restoration of custody is requested.

2. Paragraph 1.*a* of this Article also applies *mutatis mutandis* to States which have in matters of custody two or more systems of law of personal application.

### Article 27

1. Any State may, at the time of signature or when depositing its instrument of ratification, acceptance, approval or accession, declare that it avails itself of one or more of the reservations provided for in paragraph 3 of Article 6, Article 17 and Article 18 of this Convention. No other reservation may be made.

2. Any Contracting State which has made a reservation under the preceding paragraph may wholly or partly withdraw it by means of a notification addressed to the Secretary General of the Council of Europe. The withdrawal shall take effect on the date of receipt of such notification by the Secretary General.

### Article 28

At the end of the third year following the date of the entry into force of this Convention and, on his own initiative, at any time after this date, the Secretary General of the Council of Europe shall invite the representatives of the central authorities appointed by the Contracting States to meet in order to study and to facilitate the functioning of the Convention. Any member State of the Council of Europe not being a party to the Convention may be represented by an observer. A report shall be prepared on the work of each of these meetings and forwarded to the Committee of Ministers of the Council of Europe for information.

### Article 29

1. Any Party may at any time denounce this Convention by means of a notification addressed to the Secretary General of the Council of Europe.

2. Such denunciation shall become effective on the first day of the month following the expiration of a period of six months after the date of receipt of the notification by the Secretary General.

### Article 30

The Secretary General of the Council of Europe shall notify the member States of the Council and any State which has acceded to this Convention, of:

*a.* any signature;

*b.* the deposit of any instrument of ratification, acceptance, approval or accession;

*c.* any date of entry into force of this Convention in accordance with Articles 22, 23, 24 and 25;

*d.* any other act, notification or communication relating to this Convention.

In witness whereof the undersigned, being duly authorised thereto, have signed this Convention.

Done at Luxembourg, this 20th day of May 1980, in English and French, both texts being equally authentic, in a single copy which shall be deposited in the archives of the Council of Europe. The Secretary General of the Council of Europe shall transmit certified copies to each member State of the Council of Europe and to any State invited to accede to this Convention.

## BIBLIOGRAPHY OF ARTICLES ON THE UNIFORM CHILD CUSTODY JURISDICTION ACT


Bates, "UCCJA: Progress and Pitfalls," 17 Ga. S.B.J. 72 (Nov. 1980).

Belter, "Child Abductions and the UCCJA," 3 Crim. Just. J. 475 (Spring 1980).

Bodenheimer, "Judicial and Legislative Cures for Child Custody Ills," 12 Judges J. 82 (1973).

Bodenheimer, "Jurisdiction Over Child Custody and Adoption After Shaffer and Kulko," 12 U. Cal. D.L.R. 229 (1979).

Bodenheimer, "Progress Under the UCCJA and Remaining Problems: Punitive Decrees, Joint Custody, and Excessive Modifications," 65 Calif. L.R. 978 (1977).

Bodenheimer, "The International Kidnapping of Children: The United States' Approach," 11 Fam. L.Q. 83 (1977).

Bodenheimer, "The Rights of Children and the Crisis in Custody Litigation: Modification of Custody In and Out of State," 46 U. Colo. L.R. 495 (1975).

Bodenheimer, "The UCCJA," 3 Fam. L.Q. 304 (1969).

Bodenheimer, "The UCCJA: A Legislative Remedy for Children Caught in the Conflict of Laws," 22 Vand. L.R. 1207 (1969).

Buser, "At Work: The UCCJA," 23 Advocate (Idaho Bar) 5(4) (July 1980).

Cole, "Child Stealing: When to Tell a Judge Not to Exercise Jurisdiction," 1 Fam. Adv. 34 (Fall 1978).

Coombs, "The 'Snatched' Child is Halfway Home in Congress," 11 Fam. L.Q. 407 (1978).

Crouch, "The UCCJA Comes to Virginia," 27/10 Va. Bar News 22 (April 1979).

Davies, "Interprovincial Custody," 56 Can. Bar Rev. 17 (March 1978).

Davies, "Uniform Legislation: The Interstate and Interprovincial Child," 29 U. Toronto L.J. 138 (1979).

Duncan, "Child Custody: The case for Enactment of the UCCJA in Oklahoma," 33 Okla. L.R. 107 (Winter 1980).

Ehrenzweig, "Interstate Recognition of Child Custody Decrees," 51 Mich. L.R. 345 (1973).

Ehrenzweig, "The Interstate Child and Uniform Legislation: A Plea for Extralitigious Proceedings," 64 Mich. L.R. 1 (1965).

Ewaschuk, "Abduction of Children by Parents," 21 Crim. L.Q. 176 (1979).

Fain, "The Interstate Child Custody Problem Revisited," 16 ABA Fam. L. Newsl. 1 (1975).

Fleck, "Child Snatching by Parents: What Legal Remedies for 'Flee and Plea'?" 55 Chi-Kent L.R. 303 (1979).

Foster and Freed, "Child Snatching and Custodial Fights: The Case for the UCCJA," 28 Hastings L.J. 1011 (1977).

Foster and Freed, "Children and the Law," 2 Fam. L.Q. 40 (1968).

Frumkes and Elser, "UCCJA, the Florida Experience," 53 Florida Bar J. 684 (1979).

Geron, "A Brief Analysis of the UCCJA," 51 Ohio State Bar Assn. Rpt. 347 (1978).

Hoff, "Child Snatching—The Destructive Game of Hide and Seek," 1 Children's Legal Rights J. 4 (1980).

Hood, "Foreign Custody Decrees," 51 Okla. B.J. 729 (March 1980).

Hood, "Oklahoma's UCCJA," 51 Okla. B.J. 2537 (Nov. 1980).

Hudak, "Seize, Run, and Sue: The Ignominy of Interstate Child Custody Litigation in American Courts," 39 Mo. L.R. 521 (1974).

Hudak, "The Plight of the Interstate Child in American Courts," 9 Akron L.R. 257 (1975).

Jarrett, "Jurisdiction in Interstate Child Custody Disputes," 12 Gonzaga L.R. 423 (1977).

Katun and Fox, "Closing the Custody Floodgate: Florida Adopts the UCCJA," 6 Fla. St. U. L.R. 409 (1978).

Krauskopf, "Child Custody Jurisdiction Under the UCCJA," 34 Mo. B.J. 383 (1978).

Lewis, "Legalized Kidnapping of Children by Their Parents," 80 Dick L.R. 305 (1976).

Luxenberg and McLaughlin, "Child Snatching," 5/1 Dist. Law. 43 (Sep. 1980).

Lynch, "New York's New Custody Act," 51 N.Y.S.B.J. 624 (1979), and 418 N.Y.S.2d No. 2 [31] (1979).

Miller, "UCCJA: An Attempt to the Stop Child Rustling," 12 Williamette L.J. 623 (1976).

Mnookin, "Child Custody Adjudication: Judicial Functions in the Face of Indeterminacy, 39 Law and Contemp. Prob. 226 (1975).

Parker, "Representing the Parent in a 'Care and Custody' Proceeding," 57 Mass. L.Q. 387 (1972).

Podell, Peck and First, "Custody to Which Parent?" 56 Marq. L. Rev. 51 (1973).

Ratner, "Child Custody in a Federal System," 62 Mich. L.R. 795 (1964).

Ratner, "Legislative Resolution of the Interstate Child Custody Problem: A Reply to Professor Currie and a Proposed Uniform Act," 38 S. Cal. L.R. 1 (1965).

Ratner, "Procedural Due Process and Jurisdiction to Adjudicate," 75 N.W. U.L. R. 363 (1980).

Shuff, "UCCJA in Virginia," 14 U. Richmond L.R. 435 (1980).

Smith, "Commentary on Texas Family Code: Parent and Child," 8 Tex. Tech. L. Rev. 19 (1976).

Spillane, "Child Snatching," 7 Human Rights 42 (1978).

Turner, "Pennsylvania's New Child Custody Venue and Jurisdiction Legislation," 49 Penn. B.A.Q. 471 (1978).

Wallop, "Children of Divorce and Separation: Pawns in The Child-Snatching Game," 15 Trial 34 (May 1979).

Walther, "UCCJA," 54 Marq. L.R. 161 (1971).

Westbrook, "Law and Treaty Responses to International Child Abductions," 20 Va. J. Intl. L. 669 (Spring 1980).

Whicher, "Beware of the Baby Snatch," 16/4 ABA Fam. L. Newsl. 1 (Spring 1976).

NOTES:

"Child Abduction by a Relative: Maryland Enacts a Misdemeanor Offense to Deter Parental Child-Stealing," 8 U. Balt. L.R. 609 (1979).

"Child Custody Jurisdiction in Ohio—Implementing the UCCJA," 12 Akron L.R. 121 (1978).

"Children: Child Custody: The Case for Enactment of the UCCJA in Oklahoma," 33 Okla. L.R. 107 (1980).

"Children in Transit: Child Custody and the Conflict of Laws," 6 U. Cal. D. L.R. 160 (1973).

"Conflicting Custody Decrees: In Whose Best Interest?," 7 Duq. L.R. 262 (1969).

"Domestic Relations—Criminal Sanctions Against 'Child-Snatching' in North Carolina," 55 N.C.L.R. 1275 (1977).

"Due Process Dilemma of the UCCJA," 6 Ohio North. L.R. 586 (1979).

"Family Law—Child-Stealing," 6 Wm. Mitchell L.R. 461 (1980).

"Family Law: Court's Adoption of UCCJA Offers Little Hope of Resolving Child Custody Conflicts," 60 Minn. L.R. 820 (1976).

"Ford v. Ford, Full Faith and Credit to the Child Custody Decrees," 73 Yale L.J. 134 (1963).

"Jurisdiction of Texas Courts in Interstate Child Custody Disputes: A Functional Approach," 54 Texas L.R. 1008 (1976).

"Jurisdiction—UCCJA—1977 Pa. Laws No. 20 §§ 1-27," 51 Temp. L.Q. 139 (1978).

"Jurisidictional Guidelines in Matters of Child Custody: Kansas Adopts UCCJA," 27 Kan. L.R. 469 (1979).

"Oregon's Legislative Opportunity: The UCCJA," 7 Willamette L.J. 498 (Dec. 1971).
"Prevention of Child Stealing: The Need for a National Policy," 11 Loyola U. L.R. (La) 829 (1978).
"Restrictions on a Parent's Right to Travel in Child Custody Cases: Possible Constitutional Questions," 6 U. Cal. D. L.R. 181 (1974).
"Stemming the Proliferation of Parental Kidnapping: New York's Adoption of the UCCJA," 45 Brooklyn L.R. 89 (1978).
"Temporary Custody Under the UCCJA: Influence Without Modification," 48 U. Colo. L.R. 603 (1977).
"The Puzzle of Jurisdiction in Child Custody Actions," 38 U. Colo. L.R. 541 (1966).
"UCCJA," 12 U. Richmond L.R. 745 (1978).
"UCCJA in Idaho: Purposes, Application and Problems," 15 Idaho L.R. 305 (1979).
"UCCJA: Its Provision and Effects in Idaho," 7 Capital U. L.R. 453 (1978).
"UCCJA: The Difficulties it Presents for Poor People," 11 Clearinghouse R. 222 (1977).
"Use of Federal Habeas Corpus in Custody Disputes," 31 Maine L.R. 265 (1980).
"Wisconsin and the UCCJA: In Whose Hands Solomon's Sword?" 61 Marq. L.R. 79 (1977).

---

Received too late to alphabetize:
Bodenheimer, "Interstate Custody: Initial Jurisdiction and Continuing Jurisdiction under UCCJA," 14 Fam. L.Q. 203 (1981).